Before The Game

Before The Game

PHOTOGRAPHS BY SCOTT MLYN

TEXT BY LOUIS D. RUBIN, JR.

FOREWORD BY CHARLES KURALT

Taylor Publishing Company
Dallas, Texas

Published by Taylor Publishing Company
1550 West Mockingbird Lane
Dallas, Texas 75235

Grateful acknowledgment is made to the following for
permission to reprint previously published material:

Fathers Playing Catch With Sons, by Donald Hall. Copyright 1985 by North Point Press,
San Francisco.

Baseball's Greatest Quotes, compiled by Kevin Nelson. Copyright 1982 by Simon and Schuster,
New York.

Voices of Baseball, by Bob Chieger. Copyright 1983 by Atheneum, New York.

Sadaharu Oh, by Sadaharu Oh and David Falkner. Copyright 1984 by Times Books, New York.

Baseball For The Love Of It, by Anthony J. Connor. Copyright 1982 by MacMillian Publishing
Co., Inc., New York.

Sports Quotations, edited by Andrew J. Maikovich. Copyright 1984 by McFarland & Company,
Inc., Publishers, Jefferson, N.C.

Sports Quotes, by Bob Abel and Michael Valenti. Copyright 1983 by Facts on File Publications,
New York.

The Temple of Baseball, edited by Richard Grossinger. Copyright 1985 by North Atlantic
Books, Berkeley, Calif.

How Life Imitates the World Series, by Thomas Boswell. Copyright 1983 by Penguin Books,
New York. Originally published by Doubleday & Co., Inc., New York, 1982.

Library of Congress Cataloging-in-Publication Data

Mlyn, Scott.
    Before the game.

    1. Baseball — United States — Pictorial works.
2. Photography of sports. I. Rubin, Louis Decimus, 1923-   . II. Title.
        GV863.A1M58   1988   796.357'0973   88-2112
            ISBN 0-87833-605-2

Printed in the United States of America
10 9 8 7 6 5 4 3 2 1

Designed by Eisenberg, Inc.

For Lisa
S.M.

ACKNOWLEDGEMENTS

From the beginning, working on this book has been a labor of love. But in putting a project like this together, and seeing it through to publication, love alone is not enough; you also need help. Fortunately, I have had my fair share.

Firstly, I want to thank all the nice people at Taylor Publishing. In particular, recognition must be given to Dudley Jahnke, whose vision, courage and commitment have made this book a reality. Thanks also to my editor, Dominique Gioia. Her sense of judgement and diplomacy have facilitated the book's safe passage.

To Louis Rubin and Charles Kuralt, whose words have graced these pages, I am deeply grateful for your efforts. I believe yours too was a labor of love.

I would like to extend my sincere appreciation to all the major league players, managers, coaches, and trainers who opened their lives to my camera. Also, thanks to the major league public relations directors and their assistants for making the necessary arrangements.

A special thank you to my friends and family who shared their homes and hospitality with me during my journeys across the country: Mitchell Dolin, Douglas Kilgus, Mitzi and John McDonough, Rona and Jeff Moore, Dale and Rich Pilling, and Jerry Wachter. Also, for their professional guidance and assistance, thank you to David Bauer, Karen Beckers, Mary G. Burns, Andrew Christie, Roan Conrad, Arnold Dolin, Peter Gordon, Alexandra Gregson, Havlock Hughes and George Vecsey.

I am particularly pleased to acknowledge Vincent Ashbahian, whose outstanding visual talent helped create various presentations for the book, and whose generosity provided the work space necessary for the completion of this project.

Much of the credit should go to my parents: to Dad, who introduced me to both baseball and photography, and to Mom, whose unconditional love gave me the freedom to explore and find meaning.

Finally, I want to thank my loving wife Lisa, who has unfairly shared the burden of this project, but whose support and steadfast affection has carried me through.

Scott Mlyn

For their help in preparing the text for *Before the Game,* the author is indebted to his friend Walter Rabb, baseball coach emeritus at the University of North Carolina at Chapel Hill; to Clyde King, presently of the New York Yankees and before that manager of the San Francisco Giants and Atlanta Braves; and to Mike Roberts, baseball coach at the University of North Carolina at Chapel Hill.

Louis Rubin

FOREWORD

I saw my first baseball games at the old Ponce de Leon Park in Atlanta in the early '40s, and I always came early. My pal Tom Watkins and I would try to catch the Ponce de Leon streetcar by 10 in the morning on Saturdays to be there by 10:30 for the 2:00 o'clock game. It was part of our routine to climb to the top of the grandstand without looking down at the field, so that when we finally looked, we saw it all at once — the perfect diamond, home plate not yet cluttered by the batting cage, the emerald green outfield rimmed by the gaudy advertising signs, the tidy hand-operated scoreboard, and the flag — a large one — rippling over all from the flagpole above the "Buy War Bonds" sign in dead center. Old Glory nearly always fluttered toward the right field foul pole in that park. Somebody correct me if I am wrong.

But I am not wrong. I forget the details of many of the games. (Didn't the Crackers beat the Memphis Chicks three straight in August of '44 to take the league lead for the first time that summer, with Marshall Maldin, the center fielder who was an Atlanta fireman, hitting a solo home run in the tenth inning of the Saturday game to end it, and wasn't it his third homer of the game? Something like that. I was there.) I can't remember exactly what happened once the games began, but the layout of the park I remember precisely, and the slow unfolding of the pre-game ritual: the self-important teen-aged batboys solemnly placing the bats in the rack (how my pal Tom and I hated them, and wanted to BE them) while the groundskeeper limed out the foul lines with his rolling lime-liner and the pitchers ran windsprints in the outfield and a coach whacked high-bouncing, easy-to-handle grounders to the infielders, including my hero, the Cracker shortstop Ray Viers, who handled the ball so softly, around the horn to first, easy pantomime double play, the first baseman rifling the ball back to the plate, until finally it was time, and the Cracker manager, Kiki Cuyler, came shuffling out of the dugout to meet the umpires and the enemy manager to exchange lineup cards and spit some tobacco juice onto the just-raked ground, and then, just as the great Cuyler reached the top step of the dugout on his return, the players in home white rushed past him to an organ crescendo — and the announcer said, to cheers, "And the Crackers take the field!"

All that I remember perfectly.

So I think Scott Mlyn is onto something here, something about baseball that is eternal, the part of the game that occurs before the game. The players in his photographs are big leaguers, almost none of whom were born when Tom Watkins and I watched the minor league pre-game warmups of forty-five years ago. But they strike the same poses, they toss the ball with the same easy motions, they awe the little kids exactly as the Crackers did when I was one of the little kids. In these pages, a vanished team which played in a vanished time in a vanished ballpark comes back to me, and all the warmups I've watched in all the ballparks since return to my memory. Look! Winfield is in the batting cage. He still has a hitch in his swing. An hour to game time. Anything can happen here today.

Real fans all come early.

Charles Kuralt

I

BEFORE THE GAME

We arrive at the ballpark early. The ballplayers have been here for hours, for batting practice and pepper and shagging outfield flies, as coaches with fungoes bang balls at the shins of shortstops, or raise cans of corn to the shallow outfield, or strike line drives off outfield walls and corners. We arrive and settle with score cards and Crackerjack and peanuts and Schlitz and hot dogs. There is a rasp in our voice, there is glory in our infant heart, there is mustard on our T-shirt.

Donald Hall

Bag of baseballs in dugout, Fenway Park, 1986

Alejandro Peña, Dodger Stadium, 1985

Cubs playing pepper, Shea Stadium, 1984

Reggie Jackson with fan, Yankee Stadium, 1981

Yankee and fan, Yankee Stadium, 1980

Tito Landrum, Busch Stadium, 1986

Tigers taking batting practice, Tiger Stadium, 1986

Sid Bream, Shea Stadium, 1985

Photographer and player, County Stadium, 1986

Bucky Dent and Yankees playing catch, Yankee Stadium, 1979

II

THE EMPTY BALLPARK

Tiger Stadium, 1986

Yankee Stadium, 1987

When I think of a stadium, it's like a temple. It's religious.

Jim Lefebvre

. . . like those special afternoons in summer when you go to Yankee Stadium at two o'clock in the afternoon for an eight o'clock game. It's so big, so empty and so silent that you can almost hear the sounds that aren't there.

Ray Miller, coach

Yankee Stadium, 1987

Memorial Stadium in rain, 1986

Tiger Stadium in rain, 1986

The ballpark gates customarily open at least two hours before game time, but with a little ingenuity you can manage to be admitted even earlier than that. You enter the stadium and the grandstands and bleachers are all but empty. Even the concessionaires have not yet begun their rounds, although you should have been able to pick up a scorecard on your way in. It will be a long while before game time.

The visiting team is taking batting practice. If you check the numbers of the players standing around the batting cage against the roster in the scorecard you can see who is hitting. Out on the diamond, taking care to wait until after the batter in the cage has swung at a pitch, coaches are fungo-hitting ground balls for the infielders to scoop up and fire to first base. The first baseman is protected by a high rectangular screen as he takes the throws. The outfielders are grouped in the center of the outfield and another coach is hitting fly balls to them. Players on the home team, having already taken their cuts, are standing around, doing wind sprints, flexing their muscles, playing catch. Soon they will go back into the clubhouse for a meeting.

Newspaper reporters are moving about here and there, talking with players and coaches. A player or two is standing before a television camera, holding a microphone and answering questions. A pitcher is throwing along the sidelines, with the pitching coach standing by to observe and comment. There are baseballs in flight everywhere, much activity, and a great deal of talking.

It is a bright hot summer day at the ballpark, and nobody, but nobody, is in a hurry.

X

Baseball, as Dr. Joseph Garagiola has observed on more than one occasion, is a funny game. In origin it is a lower middle and working class entertainment, and for men only; indeed, in the nineteenth century and the early 1900s ladies of respectable upbringing and proper deportment would not dare be seen in a ballpark, where men drank beer, chewed tobacco, expressed their sentiments loudly in unbecoming language, and sometimes engaged in heated disputes that might even come to blows. It was commonly played by persons of little education, and such training as occurred was conducted primarily in saloons and pool halls. The majority of professional players in the early days of the game were shanty Irish and working-class English, along with some Germans, and bore colorful nicknames such as Black Jack, Boardwalk, Orator Jim, Doughnut Bill, Turkey Mike, Buttermilk Tommy, Egyptian, Steam Engine, and The Tabasco Kid. The lineup of the Chicago club of the Players League in 1890, for example, included Old Roman Comiskey, Dandelion Pfeffer, Bastian, Williamson, Duffy, Ryan, O'Neill, Duke Farrell, Honest Jack Boyle, Kid Baldwin, Silver King, Dwyer, and Arlie Lathan, known widely as "The Freshest Man on Earth."

Although the game has long since transcended its humble beginnings, certain traces of those origins still remain in its rituals and customs. There is notable absence of gentlemanly restraint and aristocratic hauteur. Players are given to violent argumentation with umpires, and spectators do not hesitate to shout insults at same, in ways that would be frowned upon in such sports as football and basketball, whose participants and audiences were for many years college-bred. The prevailing attitude toward "good sportsmanship" is mostly that it has little or nothing to do with winning baseball games. A football, basketball, tennis or golf player caught tampering with the ball or using illegal equipment would be expelled from the game in disgrace. In baseball his transgression is not only tolerated but widely admired. To be caught in the act of applying ointment to a baseball in order to make it behave erratically, or drilling a cavity in a bat and inserting cork therein in order to lighten it, occasions no public onus whatever.

Yet paradoxically, baseball holds a strong attraction for intellectuals. The ranks of its zealots include no small number of artists and savants. It has occasioned a formidable literature, and not merely because of its unique adaptation to statistics and measuring. There is that about the game that encourages imaginative absorption, and its more thoughtful devotees are routinely impelled to analyze and explain just why it is that the game appeals to them. If anyone has ever attempted a theoretical justification for football I have never read it. Where football and basketball fans are literate, baseball fans are often literary. Anyone who doubts this need only consult the catalogs of mail order sports booksellers: more books about baseball are published each year than for all other sports combined. Books like this one.

It is customary, when setting forth to pen an apologia for an addiction to our National Game, to quote Jacques Barzun, European-born literary scholar and former dean of Columbia University, to the effect that "whoever would understand the mind and heart of America must know baseball." I have no idea why this should be so; one might as plausibly declare that whoever would understand the mind and heart of America must know peanut butter, or five card stud, or Richard M. Nixon. I suspect that the reason Barzun said it, and why it is so often quoted, is that it sounds so nice. It provides rationale for a grown man who chooses to spend hours of his time watching two groups of young men taking turns trying to hit a small leather-covered ball with a round, tapered wooden club. But the simple truth, and I suspect no small part of the lure, of baseball is that *it means nothing* other than itself. To all but the club owners and the players, for whom it can offer a financial return, it exists without reference to anything else except the game itself. Three strikes make an out. Nine innings make a game. Hits, runs and errors have reference only to themselves. What are the ramifications, for our ultimate destiny prior to and reputedly beyond the grave, of a drag bunt?

No, the game of baseball is not Important, or Symbolic, or Significant. It is only endlessly and repeatedly fascinating.

Let us go then, you and I, out to the old ballpark several hours before the game is scheduled to begin, to see what we shall see.

Getting to a ballpark early, before the grandstands and bleachers fill up and the action on the field commands one's attention, offers a good opportunity to take a look at the layout of the stadium itself. Between the playing field of one major league park and another there can be enormous differences, which can drastically affect the way the game is played. Almost all baseball aficionados know about the "Green Monster" of Boston's Fenway Park, the 37-foot-high fence along Lansdowne Avenue, painted green, that lies just 305 feet away from home plate along the left-field foul line (the management claims 315 feet is the true figure) and only 379 feet in left center, and that converts pop flies into two-base hits and home runs.

Less far-famed but also of much significance, however, is the right field target at Fenway; the railing of the bleacher seats there lies at a mere 302 feet from home plate along the foul line. The field then recesses sharply in the direction of right center, the distance of which from home plate, however, is shortened by the installation of both bullpens along the outer edge.

This makes it notably easier for a left-handed batter who can pull the ball to hit even moderately well-stroked line drives into the bleacher seats for home runs, much as Mel Ott used to do for the New York Giants in the old Polo Grounds. Because of the presence of such inviting targets in Fenway, the outcome of no game played there is ever held to be certain before the final out. In the terminology of the renowned Dr. Lawrence Peter Berra, assuredly "it ain't over until it's over" at Fenway Park.

That the existence of the "Green Monster" and the truncated right-field line generally helps the home team rather than the visitors is certainly true. Not only do Red Sox left fielders acquire much skill in knowing just how to play caroms off the fence and the adjacent side of the bleachers that jut out to the left of the foul line, but the tempting proximity of the wall lures normally reasonable visiting right-handed batsmen into abandoning their customary tactics. Instead of being content to line out mere singles and doubles to all fields, they begin overswinging at pitches and undercutting them.

It has been said that just after the end of World War II, Larry MacPhail, then the head man at the New York Yankees, offered to trade the right-handed batting Joe DiMaggio to the Red Sox in exchange for the left-handed batting Ted Williams. The idea was that the famed Yankee Clipper would be able to slam shots off the Green Monster like clockwork, while Dr. Williams in turn would be able to take advantage of the nearness of the right-field bleachers in Yankee Stadium, constructed as they were to amplify the home run skills of the left-handed-batting Babe Ruth.

Fenway's contours were not originally constructed in order to favor certain kinds of hitters, but to accommodate the topographical requirements of a downtown ballpark bounded by heavily-used city streets on a lot that was and is hexagonal in shape and located between two thoroughfares that are not parallel to each other but tapering toward a merger.

The Green Monster was not always as it is today. Before 1934 there was also a ten-foot-high incline along the left-field wall, known popularly as "Duffy's Cliff" in honor of Duffy Lewis, who presided over its operations from 1912, when the stadium was built, through 1917. As a member of the Hooper-Speaker-Lewis outfield of the Red Sox during the 1910s, which oldtimers insist was the greatest ever to play the game, Lewis was a master at knowing how to play the incline and what until 1917 was only a ten-foot-high wooden fence.

Visiting left fielders, however, and subsequent Bosox performers as well, encountered much difficulty in negotiating the hill. Among the numerous legends that have grown up about the Green Monster is the one having to do with Smead Jolley. In 1932 the Sox acquired Jolley, whose entire talent was for hitting baseballs rather than catching them or running them down, and there began a two-year period of agony in the Fenway garden. Jolley, a lumbering giant of a man known to his comrades as "Smudge," had been one of the best hitters in the Pacific Coast League when brought up to the majors in 1930, and he showed that he could hit big league pitching as well. What he couldn't do, however, was to field up to major league standards.

Left field at Fenway, which despite its unique problems did not require that outfielders intervene to keep line drives from falling into the bleacher seats for home runs, seemed the safest place for the Red Sox to put Jolley when they acquired him from the White Sox. So he was given a crash course in how to sprint up the ten-foot incline in pursuit of fly balls.

There came a day, however, when Jolley, having perched himself atop the hill as directed, was required to move in quickly on a pop fly that was dropping just out of reach of the shortstop, whereupon his feet became entangled and he fell on his face. When he returned to the dugout after the inning was done, he was irate. "You told me how to climb up this &*!!**!##?**@%!! hill," he shouted, "but you didn't tell me how to get down!" Despite his hitting prowess Jolley was gone from the majors by 1934, to enjoy many additional seasons of minor league fame. Today, of course, there would be a place for Smudge Jolley in Fenway — as designated hitter.

Fenway is one of the few old-time ballparks still remaining in the major leagues, all but one of them in the American League. That the old fields, with their irregular dimensions, grass turf and dirt soil, limited seating capacity, and parking woes, are an endangered species is clear. Whatever the faults of artificial grass, it can be rapidly squeegeed off and used after a summer shower, which means that many a rain check will stay unissued during the course of a season. Most of the old parks simply do not have the seating capacity of the modern stadia, which in times of divisional championship playoffs, World Series games, and other such occasions can mean the loss of significant revenue. Among other things this can affect the size of the players' shares of the gate receipts, so that if players on a National League team in contention for the pennant and a trip to the World Series are asked whether they would prefer to go up against, say, the Boston Red Sox or the New York Yankees for the championship of the baseball world, their response will have less to do with the relative athletic merits of the two American League clubs than with the fact that Yankee Stadium seats more then 57,000 paid spectators, while Fenway can accommodate less than 34,000.

Depending on where an old-style ballpark is located, it can also face serious parking problems, and moreover the neighborhood and the means of public transport may be such that fans will be inhibited from attending games, especially at night. It is said that the decision of the New York Giants to abandon their historic bailiwick in 1958 for the West Coast was due in no small part to the increasing unwillingness of fans to traverse the area adjacent to the ballpark. Certainly the seating capacity of the Polo Grounds was not an issue; Candlestick Park, which was built for the Giants in San Francisco, can accommodate several thousand fewer patrons of the game than the older park. Once it began to be used, however, Candlestick turned out to have considerable liabilities of its own. Its location in a valley south of town and fronting the bay made it a place of dampness, cold, fog and wind. Patrons of the game learned to bring raincoats and to wear thermal underwear, especially for night games. Late each afternoon the wind usually begins blowing at a brisk rate, and in 1961 television viewers of the All-Star Game were treated to the spectacle of seeing Stu Miller, a lightly-built pitcher, literally gusted off the pitching rubber by a sudden blast of breeze.

Seating capacity *was* an important issue, however, though by no means the only one, in the simultaneous move of the Brooklyn Dodgers out to Los Angeles, for Ebbets Field, despite all its color and tradition, was limited to just over 36,000 fans, who moreover faced formidable traffic and parking problems if they wished to drive to the park instead of taking the subway. (For persons familiar with the aesthetic conditions on New York subways the dilemma will be obvious.)

The abandonment of Ebbets Field by the Dodgers has been portrayed as a crucial factor in the death of downtown Brooklyn as a sustained independent community rather than a slum area of greater New York City. What is more plausible, however, is that it was the other way around, and that Walter O'Malley and the Dodger management realized that the area around the banks of the Gowanus Canal in Flatbush was already going rapidly downhill. In any event, the ballpark that O'Malley built in Chavez Ravine in suburban Los Angeles was accessible by freeway, had vast acres of space for paid parking, and could seat more than 56,000 persons.

I remember once, years ago, driving over with a friend to Connie Mack Stadium (the once and future Shibe Park) in Philadelphia to attend a Phillies game at night. The adjacent parking lots were all filled, and we found a parking place on a street some five or six blocks from the park. As we got out of the car several youths offered, for a consideration, to keep an eye on our car. We did not yield to the attempted blackmail, and when we returned after the game the car had not been harmed, but throughout the intervening three hours there was the uncomfortable knowledge that if we came back to the car to find the tires flattened or slashed, there would be almost no chance of the culprits being located and apprehended. I have never attended a game in Veterans Stadium, which in 1971 replaced Shibe Park as the home of the Phillies, but my guess is that if I did I would discover ample paid parking space, to the profit of the ball club and the benefit of my peace of mind.

The advantages of the old-style parks — Fenway in Boston, Comiskey Park and Wrigley Field in Chicago, Tiger Stadium (formerly Navin and Briggs Field) in Detroit — are principally aesthetic. They were designed exclusively or principally for baseball, and the resulting closeness to the field of play makes the game more intimate to watch. (Recently I attended a night game at Arlington Stadium in Texas. From our seats at the very top of the grandstand behind home plate the Texas Rangers and the visiting New York Yankees were so far away that it was all we could do to read the numbers on the backs of the uniforms.) Certainly there is the aura of Tradition with which the old parks are richly coated: and major league baseball is a game of historical continuity.

To look out upon the diamond at Tiger Stadium, built as it was in 1912, and to know that Tyrus Raymond Cobb, his hands spread wide on the handle of his bat, once intimidated American League pitchers right out there before one's eyes, is to indulge the historical sense validly and harmlessly. Pretend that the Tiger playing first base is not Darrell Evans but Hank Greenberg (the white uniform with the gothic "D" on it looks almost exactly the same as in Greenberg's day). Pretend that Charlie Gehringer is at second base. Or pretend that waiting on deck to hit behind Cobb is Wahoo Sam Crawford himself, while the manager standing in the dugout is not Sparky Anderson but Hugh Jennings or Black Mike Cochrane. Why not?

To be able to compare the point of departure of one of Darryl Strawberry's home runs over the center-field wall in Wrigley Field with one of Willie Mays', or Hack Wilson's, and to know that both occurred right there where one is now looking, can nurture the imagination. To imagine that Shoeless Joe Jackson is playing outfield in Comiskey Park is no great feat for the ballfan with what Hemingway called *afición*.

A telling aesthetic argument against the new parks is that with few exceptions they look almost identical to one another. Most are symmetrical, with the distances down the foul lines and the power alleys identical in left and right field. The grass is artificial and dyed. The seats are plastic and pastel, as against the comfortable, aged forest green of the wooden seats in the old parks. There are no painted signs on outfield fences announcing that Karl Karesh Clothiers will award a new suit to any home team player hitting a ball over it on the fly, or that gentlemen should "FOR COMFORT SAKE — DEMAND B.V.D. LOOSE-FITTING UNDERWEAR." As Dr. Richie Hebner, recently of the Pittsburgh Pirates and other clubs, remarked of Veterans Stadium in Philadelphia, "I stand at the plate in Philadelphia and I don't honestly know whether I'm in Pittsburgh, Cincinnati, St. Louis, or Philly. They all look alike."

The quotation just cited appears in *Green Cathedrals,* by Philip J. Lowry, a highly informative volume giving the history and details of all major league and many minor league ballparks past and present, published in 1986 by the Society for American Baseball Research. There is something of a tendency among certain literary baseball fans to refer to baseball fields as cathedrals or temples, meaning inferentially that they are intended for purposes of worship. Doubtless the singing of the National Anthem before the start of a game is supposed to correspond to the Introit, while the playing of "Take Me Out to the Ball Game" is the equivalent of "Tantum Ergo Sacramentum," the Doxology, or the "Kol Nidrei," depending upon one's denominational affiliation.

All who wish to approach the watching of major league baseball as a branch of theology have my permission to do it, but it has always struck me as being just a mite on the extravagant side. It is difficult to conceive of the purchase and consumption of lager beer in plastic cups, for example, as appropriate conduct for a communicant seated in a cathedral, nor am I able to equate such secular melodies as "Three Blind Mice," "Alley Cat," and "The Colonel Bogey March," as rendered over the PA system, with the singing of a high mass. Besides, if the religious analogy is to govern, then the balls-and-strikes umpire would have to be the officiating celebrant, and the umpires on the bases his assistants. What, though, is the liturgical role of such distinguished umpire-crawlers as Earl Weaver, Billy Martin, and Tommy Lasorda?

What I believe accounts in large part for the fervor with which poets, pundits, and college pro-

fessors feel compelled to rhapsodize about it is that they were young when they themselves engaged in it. Baseball was customarily played during the last spring and the summer months, when school was either soon to let out or closed for the summer vacation. As players of sandlot baseball the future literati had not yet entered into the full specialization of intellectual labor, and were not thereby culturally set apart from the larger middle-class community.

Watching baseball, therefore, offers them a temporary return to a time when the weather was warm and good, the nights were long, the schoolhouse door was locked for the summer, and one's friends and companions did not yet consist principally of other highly specialized scholars, writers, scientists, savants and so on. Whatever their occupational, social, and cultural separateness, as baseball fans from the Pulitzer Prize-winning poet, the R.F.D. deliveryman, the atomic physicist, the automobile mechanic, and the real estate salesman all spoke and can still speak the same language. To justify such activity to that portion of oneself which is concerned with Higher Things, Fenway Park is made into the Cathedral of St. Theodore the Splendid and the Blessed Carl Yastzremski, Shea Stadium into the Conventicle of St. Dwight, Comiskey Park into the Chapel of St. Luke of Appling, Tiger Stadium into Temple Beth Greenberg, Busch Stadium into the Abbey of the Sainted Fr. Herzog, Wrigley Field into a shrine to James Vaughn, Bishop of Hippo, and so on. It is our way.

To return to the subject at hand, the one kind of contemporary baseball park that is said to represent a truly drastic departure from all previous emporia is the enclosed or domed stadium, of which the Houston Astrodome was first. That baseball played under a roof can affect the nature of the game is obvious. All those who witnessed the 1987 World Series between the St. Louis Cardinals and the Minnesota Twins can testify to how much difference playing in the Twins' Metrodome made. The white ceiling caused extreme difficulty for the visiting Redbirds, accustomed as they were to observing long fly balls against a backdrop of sky, when they needed to pick up the flight of baseballs hit toward them in the enclosed air. The acoustics of the enclosed Metrodome resulted in audial bedlam; Cardinal infielders and outfielders could not call each other off of fly balls, and the din made it extremely difficult for anyone not accustomed to it to concentrate his attention.

Houston's Astrodome and Seattle's Kingdome would appear not to be quite so heavily weighted against the visiting team. In the former, however, the enclosed, air-conditioned atmosphere, in conjunction with the excessive length of the power alleys along each foul line, seems to work against the hitting of home runs. Annually the facility leads the majors in the fewest of fair balls hit into the stands, and annually the resident Astros have the lowest home run production in either league.

The big advantage of an enclosed field is its virtual immunity to the postponement of scheduled games because of rain, snow, cold, wet grounds, or extreme heat. Let no one dismiss this as of no importance. Baseball games are meant to be seen and enjoyed. It may be easy for those who live in close proximity to a major league franchise to denounce baseball in roofed stadia as a crime against nature. But someone who must drive a hundred miles and more from out in the provinces to see a major league baseball game, only to have it cancelled because of the weather, is likely to have little patience with the high-minded purist for whom viewing a ball game means no more than a brief journey via mass transit, and who can decide to attend or not to attend a scheduled game in accordance with weather forecasts made an hour before game time.

Anyone who witnessed the 1979 World Series between the Pittsburgh Pirates and the Baltimore Orioles will remember the sub-freezing conditions in Baltimore's Memorial Stadium, and how the performing athletes slipped and stumbled their way through the first two games. There was a one-day postponement of the opening game because of heavy rain, and it snowed the next morning. When the heavens let up sufficiently to permit the Series to start, fans were treated to an error-plagued contest played in light rain, with snow and ice on the edges of the field and the temperature in the lower 40s. The next day's game was scarcely much better. It was simply not baseball as it should be played; had the games been scheduled inside an enclosed stadium the quality of play would have been vastly enhanced. Now that the best-out-of-seven-game divisional playoffs have moved the Series dates into late October, one wonders what is going to happen when, as will surely happen eventually, the Mets or Cubs get involved in a Series against Milwaukee or Toronto or Boston, and several days of rain or snow are followed by a Canadian high, sending the temperatures down into the teens or twenties. Will the Commissioner of Baseball move the remaining games out to Jack Murphy Stadium in San Diego? Even without playoffs the 1911 World Series didn't get over until October 26.

So it can work both ways. As one who has often watched as many as seventy-five to a hundred games a season, including sandlot, college, semipro, minor league and major league contests, and not counting games seen on television, I would far rather attend a baseball game played indoors than outdoors on days when it is bitterly cold and windy, or when the mercury is in the high nineties and not a breath of air is blowing, or when a thunderstorm is about to arrive and cause a lengthy delay or even cancellation of the game in progress, or when the same has passed on after depositing a number of wading pools in the outfield, and so on. Aesthetic considerations are best weighed when the body is at ease.

The team batting practice that takes place before a game — at least two hours and ten minutes before for the home team, an hour and a half before for the visitors — is not designed to perfect skills or to correct flaws, but to allow the player to get the rhythm of his swing down, so that when he comes to bat during a game he will not be hitting cold. Before either team hits, the players will have gone through a series of stretching exercises designed to prepare the leg and arm muscles for activity. When the hitting begins, the ball is thrown in either by a coach or a special batting practice pitcher. It will be noted that the person doing the throwing works from behind a screen, with one half of the top portion of the netting open to permit the pitch to be delivered, following which the pitcher can duck behind the raised segment and be safe from line drives. This is because the batter is expected to hit the ball — solidly and hard. The pitcher tosses it in right down the middle of the plate, grooving it so that a batter of any competence cannot miss connecting with it. The velocity of the pitch is scarcely more than 50 to 60 miles an hour. What is being practiced is not the ability to hit good pitching, but the rhythm of the swing. Any batting practice pitcher who tried to throw strikes, to make the batter swing and miss, would be speedily removed from the mound, because the objective is to let the batter hit the ball, and the harder the better.

To observe a baseball being hit is the primary and elemental attraction of the game. Pre-game batting practice, with one player after another stepping into the batting cage and attempting to whale the daylight out of a pitched ball, is a satisfying affair to view, the more so if the viewer knows who the individual batters are. An Atlanta Braves fan, for example, may watch his heroes step up to the plate one after the other and swing away. Dion James drives three shots into the left-field corner. Ken Oberkfell goes with the pitch, lines four base hits to left field. Dale Murphy sends a pair of awesome fly balls far beyond the center-field fence 402 feet distant from the plate. And so on. In batting practice everybody hits the ball.

✕

One of the legends of major league baseball concerns the batting practice that the 1927 New York Yankees took the day before the first game of the World Series against the Pittsburgh Pirates. The sluggers of the New York Murderers Row, who had pounded out the then-unprecedented total of 158 home runs during a regular season that saw them finish 19 games in front of the second-place Athletics, proceeded to display their might. This was the year that Babe Ruth hit 60 home runs, and there was also Lou Gehrig with 47 and Tony Lazzeri with 18. Ruth had driven in no less than 164 runs, and Gehrig 175, while Lazzeri had 102 and Bob Meusel 103. The Yankees were big men physically, especially for their day — Ruth was 6′2″, Meusel 6′3″, Gehrig and Earle Combs 6′, and Lazzeri 5′11½″.

By contrast, the Pirates, who had squeaked through to win the National League pennant by a mere game-and-a-half over the second-place St. Louis Cardinals, had no player in the lineup who had hit as many as 10 home runs. Their best hitters were the diminutive Waner Brothers, Paul and Lloyd, and Pie Traynor, Paul Waner was all of 5′8½″, and his brother Lloyd only a half-inch taller. Clyde Barnhart was 5′10″, first baseman Joe Harris 5′9″, shortstop Glenn Wright 5′11″. Traynor, the third baseman, was the big man of the outfit at six feet.

What happened, the legend goes, is that the Yankees put on a demonstration of home run hitting that threw the Pirates into shell shock. As their batting practice pitchers grooved balls to their liking, they drove shot after shot into the grandstands, with the result that the Pirates were thoroughly cowed, and New York won the Series in a four-game sweep. Whether in actuality the Pirates were inhibited by what they saw that day is dubious; they denied it emphatically then and later, and given the nature of batting practice pitching and hitting it seems unlikely. But it is the only occasion on record in which hitting prowess during a pre-game batting practice is supposed to have affected the outcome of a World Series.

✕

The real hitting *practice* — as distinguished from the lining out of shots to get the batter's rhythm properly set — takes place many hours before the start of a game, in the morning, or if it is a night game early in the afternoon. It is then that certain players will come out to work on their hitting with the team batting coach. The complex fusion of stance, grip, stride, and swing, with the required split-second adjustment to each individual pitch, whether high, low, inside, outside, fastball or curve, slider or knuckler, that takes place each time a batter swings at a thrown baseball, is nothing to be tampered with during a game itself. Nor is there time for experimentation or remedial instruction at pre-game batting practice, with others awaiting their turn in the batting cage. The objective is simply to get the rhythm of hitting a baseball sufficiently under control. At such times the emphasis is on the fluid motion of the complete effort, as an entity in itself. The time for taking the swing apart, subjecting its numerous component parts to critical scrutiny, is when there is no rush, no pressure, so that batter and hitting instructor can patiently go through swing after swing, looking for hidden flaws, subtle and unsuspected little movements or compensations that can throw off the timing and effectiveness of the hitting motion.

Nowadays major league teams make a practice of collecting ample videotape footage on all their players when they are at bat. What they want to be able to do is to observe the batter's swing at a time when he is hitting well, so that when he runs into a slump and cannot buy or borrow a basehit, what he is doing or failing to do at the plate can be compared with the way he batted when he was getting his hits. So seemingly slight a change as dropping an elbow ever so slightly when awaiting a pitch, or flexing a knee a trifle when turning into the ball, or striding a couple of inches further than usual when he is chasing a breaking ball, can throw a batter's swing completely out of kilter, distort his follow-through, and render a hitherto-menacing hitter all but impotent.

It is the batting coach's job to observe those little things, spot the seemingly insignificant flaws, and work with the batter at correcting them. It is also the coach's job to recommend changes, sometimes drastic ones, in the batting styles of players who are unable to hit consistently and effectively. Depending on the personality of the batting coach in question, such changes can be made as a result

of a theory as to what constitutes a fundamentally sound approach to hitting, or more pragmatically, as the individual batter's particular needs may dictate.

The late Charlie Lau, for example, believed very strongly that batters should use at least a closed stance, with the front foot on a line with or even a bit closer to the plate than the rear foot. He wanted his charges to use the whole field when they hit, going with the pitch instead of attempting to pull every ball. They would hit just as many home runs that way, he insisted, as when they sought to get the bat fully around on every pitch and drive it over the fence. The batter should hit through the ball, not try to uppercut it and jerk it out of the park. Under the Lau system a good follow-through was essential; the batter should bring the bat fully around after his swing, releasing his upper hand from the grip to let the bat complete its arc.

The teams on which Lau functioned as batting instructor soon came to bear the imprint of his theories, which he incorporated in a book entitled *The Art of Hitting .300*. His star pupil, George Brett of the Kansas City Royals, who came close to being the first major leaguer to top the .400 mark as a hitter since Ted Williams did it in 1941, is a perfect exemplar of his method. Brett ended the 1980 season hitting a solid .390. When Hal McRae joined the Royals in 1973 he was a good fastball hitter but had trouble with curves. Lau moved him back from the plate, had him cut back on his stride, and taught him to control his swing more instead of going all-out after the long ball. The result was that McRae became a steady .300 hitter

— and ended up hitting more home runs than ever before.

Lau himself was not a notably successful hitter during his major league career; playing usually as a back-up catcher, he had a lifetime batting average of only .255. But as so often happens, the best practitioners are not necessarily the best teachers; it is the less naturally gifted player, who cannot rely upon instinct and habit but must work constantly and strenuously at his trade, striving to make the maximum possible use of his limited talents, who comes to understand the fundamental principles of what he and all other players are engaged in doing, and so can best impart them to others.

One of the more successful pitching coaches, Jim Turner, was 34 years old before he made it up to the major leagues after long years in the minors. Turner enjoyed one season, his first, as a twenty-game winner, and thereafter was for eight seasons a journeyman pitcher at best, winning only 69 games in all while losing 60. Yet as a pitching coach Turner was able to impart his hard-won skills to other and more naturally gifted pitchers, not a few of whom proceeded to enjoy far more distinguished careers that he ever did.

It doesn't always work that way, however. Johnny Sain was a top-line pitcher for the Boston Braves, four times winning twenty games or more in a season. "Spahn and Sain . . . and pray for rain," it used to be said, in reference to the fact that the Braves of the post-World War II years had relatively little in the way of good pitching to follow Sain and Warren Spahn. As a coach Sain was, if anything, even more outstanding than as a pitcher. For years every major league pitching staff that came under his tutelage blossomed forth with twenty-game winners. Sain's coaching method was as much psychological as technical; he set out to gain the full confidence of the pitchers he worked with, and did it so successfully that ultimately the team manager would begin to resent the way that his pitchers looked to Sain for guidance rather than to himself. Again and again Sain developed outstanding pitchers, only to be fired from his job.

By and large, however, the most successful batting and pitching coaches, as well as team managers, have not been drawn from the ranks of the game's superstars. The late Rogers Hornsby, for example, considered by many the greatest right-handed batter in baseball history, was not an especially successful manager and teacher of hitters, both because he was unable to comprehend the needs of players who did not possess his own superlative natural skills and because he was temperamentally incapable of realizing that what had worked so well for him might not work equally well for other players of different personalities and capacities.

When Hornsby took over as manager of the Chicago Cubs toward the close of the 1930 season, he inherited a team whose foremost ornament was 5′6″ Hack Wilson, the most feared power hitter in the National League. In 1930 Wilson set an all-time major league record of 190 runs batted in, and an all-time National League record of 56 home runs. But in the season following, 1931,

Wilson's batting average dropped 95 points from .356 to .261, with a bare 13 homers and only 61 runs driven in.

The sudden and precipitous decline puzzled everyone. "What's happened to Wilson?" a player on another team asked one of the Cubs. "Hornsby's taken the bat out of his hands," he was told. It seems that Hornsby, whose eye for the strike zone was so keen that it was said that he got four strikes every time he came to bat, had given orders that all Chicago Cub batters were to take the first pitch rather than swing at it, no matter how attractive the pitch might look to them. For the roly-poly, free-swinging Wilson, whose way of hitting had been to step into the box and whale away zestfully at whatever was offered, Hornsby's dictum was baffling, and so inhibited his performance at the plate that he lost both his confidence and much of his pleasure in hitting, and never afterward regained his onetime prowess at the plate. A formidable drinker, he took to the bottle as never before, and was soon gone from the majors for good.

A great deal more and better hitting and pitching instruction, as well as pre-game physical conditioning, goes on in professional baseball nowadays than in years past. The stretching exercises used before beginning practice, for example, are a post-World War II innovation, popularized first by Bob Feller. The Cleveland right-hander had a whole set of conditioning exercises he used before beginning to throw, and ultimately the various

teams began to copy his lead. For decades the attitude toward coaching taken by most major league clubs was that it was the player's responsibility, not the team's, to find out how to do his job satisfactorily; by the time the player reached the major leagues he ought to *know* how. (The fact that, unlike the custom in other professional sports such as football and basketball, the man in charge of a professional baseball team is called the manager rather than the coach is a survival of this earlier attitude.) The idea of a team employing an instructor to help players hit or pitch was absurd. The same was true in the minor leagues; a young player learned by watching and by experimentation, and occasionally from an older teammate. The latter, however, frequently took the position that a rookie who was joining the team was a threat to his own job or that of his friends, and he was going to do nothing to aid him in that enterprise.

Ethan Allen, a lifetime .300 hitter in thirteen seasons of major league play, and afterward a long-time college baseball coach at Yale, tells of his first spring training trip with the Cincinnati Reds in 1927. He had joined the team directly from college the summer before, and he was looking forward eagerly to the hitting and fielding instruction he would get at the Reds' training camp in Florida. To his dismay he found that nobody taught anything to anyone; the sole purpose of spring training was to enable the players to get into top physical condition for the ensuing season.

Allen, whose *Baseball Play and Strategy* has long been considered one of the finest instructional books on playing baseball, tells a story that characterizes the attitude of so many old-time ballplayers toward teaching the game. When Bill McKechnie was manager of the Cincinnati Reds in the late 1930s, the veteran catcher and ex-Philadelphia Phillies manager Jimmie Wilson was serving as coach. On one occasion the Reds lost a game as the result of a horrendous job of baserunning. In an effort to have the team brush up on its technique when running the bases, Wilson offered to stage a clinic on that subject. McKechnie declined emphatically. "If they can't run the bases," he declared, "we'll get some players who can."

Not all major league players held that attitude, of course. There were numerous instances of older players volunteering their services to help promising youngsters. In 1947, when Ralph Kiner was in his second season with the Pittsburgh Pirates, the veteran Hank Greenberg joined the club. It was Greenberg's custom to take hours of extra batting practice, and he soon had Kiner practicing along with him. "We'd shag for each other and have different people pitch to us," Kiner told Donald Honig. "He changed my stance and my whole approach to hitting — taught me to hit for power — and I jumped from twenty-three home runs in 1946 to fifty-one in 1947, the year he came."

Especially after the major league baseball teams began developing farm systems in the 1920s and 1930s, the situation began changing. When teams began to contract for hundreds of young prospects and to operate minor league teams composed exclusively of their own players, it made good sense to hire managers for these teams with some ability to teach their young players to master the basic skills of the game, and special batting and pitching instructors to circulate about the farm system to work with prospective major league players. Today, when the minor leagues are made up entirely of farm clubs, and the contracts for all players are owned by the major league teams, the emphasis is entirely upon preparing young players for the majors, and even the high minors are in effect teaching academies.

Even before that it was the custom, back in the days when eligibility rules for amateur athletics were considerably less rigid, for major league clubs to pay the college tuition and expenses of certain likely prospects so that they could learn the fundamentals from selected college coaches. When the former Philadelphia Athletics pitcher Jack Coombs, for example, was baseball coach at Duke University, there was a steady stream of good young players learning their trade on Coombs' teams, and who then just happened to end up with professional contracts with the Athletics. A number of college and university baseball coaches had similar "understandings" with major league clubs.

Each major league team has its regimen for pre-game hitting. Everybody on the roster except those pitchers who are not likely to be used that day gets his swings; in the American League, of course, with its designated hitter, the only time that pitchers ever have the chance to bat is in World Series games, and then only in the National

League park. Usually the pitchers hit first, followed by those players who will not be in the lineup that day, and after that the starting lineup. Each team gets forty minutes for batting practice. Most teams have each player take two bunts and five swings, although early in the season each batter practices hitting behind the runner as well. After that, the batter gets to swing away as he wishes, with strikes and foul balls counting equally with fair balls, and sometimes he runs the last one out. If the batter is a switch hitter he may elect to try several swings from either side of the plate. If he is fast afoot and likes to drag a bunt down the line for a hit, he does so on the last pitch.

Batting practice moves along at a brisk pace, with another batter waiting to move into the cage as soon as the preceding batter is done. Depending upon how much of the alloted forty minutes remains, the regulars may bat around two or three times or even more often. The batting practice pitcher delivers pitch after pitch, with just enough time between tosses to allow the batter to get set for the next pitch. Several players are usually assigned to stand behind the pitcher and collect the baseballs that are thrown back in by the fielders. A wire bin of baseballs is kept at the pitcher's side, elevated just high enough so that he need only reach over and extract a ball to throw. In all this procedure there is seldom a wasted motion; the forty minutes of alloted hitting time must be used to maximum benefit.

The ability to pitch batting practice is, if not an art, then a skill that not all can master. The pitcher must deliver pitch after pitch into the strike zone, with few misses. The ball must be thrown at about three-quarter speed — fast enough to allow the batter to set his timing for the game, yet not so fast that it is difficult to hit. The batter expects to get both high and low pitches. Most of the major league clubs use non-roster pitchers employed especially for this purpose — the New York Yankees, for example, have two left-handers and two right-handers on the payroll strictly for batting-practice pitching — while several of the team's coaches are also expected to be adept at it. Sometimes, too, a retired pitcher who happens to be in town will suit up and throw batting practice; and in more than one major league city some of the team's radio and television broadcasters who were formerly players in their own right will throw. At least four pitchers are required for the forty minutes of continuous throwing, and depending upon which opposing pitcher is scheduled to start that day, the final practice pitching will usually be right- or left-handed, while if the opponent is known to make heavy use of a particular pitch, such as a sinker or a slider, there may be an effort made to supply samples of that kind of pitch to hit against before the game.

Watching batting practice, like taking it, can be a considerable pleasure. The players for the most part are loose, relaxed, and enjoying it — for hitting a baseball, as every youth baseball coach knows, is what is most fun. However, the procedure can be very revealing. For it is no coincidence that the players who do the best job of bunting are usually those who also do the best job of hitting behind the runner. To do so requires considerable precision, and also no small amount of patience. It is possible to identify which of the players on a team possess the kind of thoroughgoing professional dedication to baseball as a demanding vocation, and which ones are less strongly motivated. The real professionals on the team will invariably look on bunting and the need to practice place hitting not as a nuisance to be gotten over before they are free to swing for the fences, but as the opportunity to perfect a skill that if mastered can win close ball games. Even though a power hitter such as a Carl Yastrzemski or a Dale Murphy will almost never be called upon in a game to sacrifice a base runner to second, he will take pride in being able to lay down a bunt along the baseline so precisely that an on-charging first or third baseman will have to field it, rather than the pitcher or catcher, thus giving the runner ample time to move up. Conversely, those players who are possessed of natural hitting skills but are impatient with such unglamorous chores are less likely to develop into the long-term stars of the game.

For most players, the opportunity to hit away in batting practice becomes a kind of intramural competition, and they enjoy vying with each other to see who can drive the ball furthest and most authoritatively. One after another they move into the batting cage to take their cuts, and the fan can watch as shot after shot goes sailing toward the stands and to the far corners of the outfield, and if sufficiently observant note the characteristics of each player's swing.

Nor will the fans alone be observing closely. On the bench of the opposing team, chances are that the manager, coaches, catchers, and pitchers will be watching, too. It will not be long before they will be faced with the need to decide which pitches to throw to those batters, and which pitches not to use as well. If the young rookie in the batting cage who is currently making headlines for his sensational hitting smashes a waist-high fastball into the stands but on the next pitch looks a trifle awkward in adjusting to a slider that comes in low and outside, when he comes to bat in a game he may well find himself first getting a fastball thrown close in to his body but out of the strike zone, and then a slider down and away. Each team has a "book," whether written down, carried in the manager's head, or both, on the batting habits of all other players in the league, but it must be constantly updated, and what happens in batting practice can provide useful additional information.

While the pre-game batting practice goes on, coaches will be hitting fly ball after fly ball, not only to the outfielders but to the pitchers as well. The ease with which a skilled fungo hitter can knock out long, looping fly balls belies the considerable skill involved in the endeavor. Fungo hitting is a minor art form, and early arrivals at the game take much pleasure from watching its execution. Although a few practitioners prefer to use regular model baseball bats, most employ a special bat known as an outfield fungo — long, with a thin barrel, resembling a softball bat except that the handle is much thinner and the taper to the barrel less gradual. Customarily the barrel of the fungo is wrapped with several layers of adhesive tape, which not only preserves the bat longer but cushions the impact on the ball and provides greater control.

The master of the fungo fly is the legendary Jimmy Reese, who although in his eighties was renowned for his talent with the outfield fungo. Reese was a reserve infielder for the New York Yankees in 1930 and 1931, and on road trips was roommate to Babe Ruth. Born James Hymie Solomon in 1904, he changed his name because of the considerable anti-Semitism that was prevalent when he broke into baseball. Reese has been a coach for the California Angels during the 1970s and 1980s, with the special responsibility of keeping the club's pitchers in good physical condition by hitting fungo flies just out of their reach. Seemingly with little effort, Reese could loft a baseball across 300 feet of outfield turf to a designated spot, forcing the pitcher to sprint over and take it on the run. So adept was he with fungo and ball that he could actually "pitch" batting practice with the fungo bat, swatting fastballs into the strike zone with almost pinpoint accuracy.

When batting practice for both teams is done, it is time to take infield. On signal, the home team's players sprint out onto the diamond and assume the positions they will play that day or may if substituted.

Until now all has been leisurely and easy-going. From that moment on, however, the tempo of practice changes. Everyone begins to hustle. Baseballs are no longer lobbed, but thrown with velocity. A coach, sometimes even the manager himself, emerges from the dugout with a bat and baseballs, and sets up his headquarters to one side of the pitching mound. A catcher moves up alongside him, while another stations himself at home plate.

The coach begins hitting to the outfielders, first to left, then to center, then to right. He hits a fairly easy ball down the left-field line, which the fielder takes and throws to second base to hold an imagined runner to a single. Next comes another designed to be fired to the third baseman to prevent a runner from going from first to third on a base hit. Then a ball is hit on the ground through the hole between third and short, which the left-fielder charges and pegs home to keep a runner from scoring.

Everyone is paying strict attention now; there is no loafing. The throws are being made exactly as if the game were in progress. As the left fielder's throw comes in toward the catcher, the first baseman moves across the diamond to intercept it. If the throw is on target the catcher will call to him to let it come through; if it is off the line he will shout "Cut!" and the first baseman will cut it off. When the left-fielders are done the center-fielders take over with the same routine, and after them the right-fielders.

Now it is the infield's turn, and the real fun begins. The coach moves back to the home plate area, and the catchers stand behind him to take turns. The routine is rapid now, following a prescribed order. The coach, who has hit thousands of ground balls in his time, can place the ball exactly where he wants it. If he so wishes he can slap out what the trade refers to as a "zazoo" — an undercut ball which will skip and slice off the turf and give the infielder fits. But the object is to make the infielders look good, and instead he is likely to knock out what is called a "gallop" or a "Big Bill" — a ball that is topped so that it bounces high and true.

The first ball goes to the infielder's glove side. "Get one!" The third baseman scoops up a grounder, fires to first. The first baseman in turn fires home. The catcher fires to third — no looping throws these, but as hard as the arm can propel the ball. The third baseman takes the throw, moves as if to tag a sliding runner, then throws to the second baseman, who throws to the first baseman, who throws home. It is *Wham! Bam! Thank You Ma'am!* all the way, with everyone shouting.

Next the shortstop — a hard grounder, which if he miscues will be followed by another, and another, until he gets it right. Short to first to catcher to short to third to catcher. Second to first to catcher to short to third to catcher. First to short to first to catcher. The coach rolls a simulated bunt along the first base line, the catcher leaps upon it, fires to first, from where it goes to the shortstop, then back to the catcher.

"Get one!" A second time around, the ball hit to the infielder's left this time. "Get two!" The ball goes "around the horn" — hit on the ground to the third baseman, who throws to second, who throws to first for the double play, and then to home, to third, to first, and back home again. "Get two!" Another round of same. "Get one!" "Get one!"

On the final go-around each infielder gets a ground ball to throw to first, races in to field a bunt on the run and flip it to the catcher, then continues in to the dugout on the run, to sit down, panting, and catch his breath. It has been a frantic ten minutes, with throw after throw, with shouts and yells and talking it up, designed to quicken the tempo, sharpen the reflexes, get the adrenalin flowing. It concludes with a high pop fly lofted straight overhead by the coach for the catcher to take — provided, that is, the coach can hit it straight up and near enough to home plate. Then it is the visiting team's turn.

To knowledgeable devotees of the game of baseball, infield practice is a treat indeed. To watch so many gifted athletes in motion at all-out speeds, scooping up hard infield shots, setting themselves, firing balls at outstretched gloves and mitts, pivoting, turning, stretching, and all the while shouting and calling encouragement to each other, is not just to view a practice session, but to witness a kind of pantomime of an almost dancelike grace and precision. A rhythm is established, a tempo achieved. It is play, yet done in dead earnest. And if the observer is familiar with the individual ability of the various players, he soon learns to anticipate how each will perform, and compare their tactics. The best infielders make it look incredibly easy, wasting no motion as they execute their assignments.

What the really great infielders have is restraint. An Ozzie Smith, a Brooks Robinson, a Luis Aparicio, a Marty Marion, a Frank White, a Pie Traynor seems not to hurry or strain to reach the ball; he is simply there when the ball arrives, glove held low and waiting, and when he rises to throw it is done in one fluid motion, the ball is unleashed without fuss, always in time to beat the runner, yet seemingly never with excessive effort.

It is the speed of release that is so marvelous. National League players in the 1930s used to say, for example, that Traynor got rid of the ball from third base so quickly that Gus Suhr, the Pirates' first baseman, had to hustle frantically to get to the bag in time to receive it. And the millions of televison viewers who have seen the Cardinals' Ozzie Smith make acrobatic throws in mid-air, without even setting himself first, know why even oldtimers who normally insist that today's major leaguers are not up to the standards of the great players of the past usually make an exception in favor of Ozzie. There is nobody else quite like him.

When both the home and visiting clubs have completed their infield practice, the players leave the field. The grounds crew now takes over. Unless the infield is of artificial turf with only the areas around the bases having dirt surface, as in Cincinnati's Riverfront Stadium or the Minnesota Twins' Metrodome, the most important job is to drag the infield, rake it, and then lightly hose it down. The combined steel cleats of two ball clubs taking batting and fielding practice will have thoroughly scuffed the surface, which must be made sufficiently smooth to allow ground balls to bounce cleanly. The area around home plate must be worked over carefully, and the holes where batters have dug in their heel spikes to get a firm foundation for swinging at pitches must be filled in. The pitcher's mound must also get a careful raking, in particular the area in front of the slab, because any unevenness in the surface can cause a pitcher to lose his balance when he strides forward to deliver the ball to the plate.

A connoisseur of baseball playing fields — there are some — can take considerable pleasure in watching the operations of a grounds crew. It is a precision performance, and the participants are drilled at it until they know how to play their parts perfectly. Nowadays they are uniformed and work in something close to cadenced command.

It used to be that considerable latitude was allowed groundskeepers in preparing the infield and elevating the mound. Over the years the height of the pitcher's slab in some ballparks was elevated to such proportions that batters had to cope with pitches that seemed to come sailing down from on high; with good reason sports writers might refer to the pitcher's box as "the hill." Conditions grew so extreme in this respect by the 1960s that the traditional "balance" between batting and pitching was being endangered. Batting averages were dipping alarmingly. In 1968 Carl Yastrzemski's American League-leading batting average was only .301, and no other hitter in the league hit as high as .300. So the rule book was amended so that all major league mounds were set at a uniform ten inches.

There were, and no doubt still are, all manner of "improvements" that a groundskeeper and his crew can make that will give the home team an advantage. If a visiting team was known for its speed afoot, while the home team goes for the long ball and the big inning, the infield dirt near the bases can be softened up, making it more difficult for would-be base stealers to get a good jump. Conversely, if the home team has some speedsters in its lineup the ground can be tightly packed and a supply of clay worked in with the soil, thereby improving conditions at the launching pad. If the home team goes in for lots of bunting, the edge of the base paths along the foul lines can be built up ever so slightly, so that a bunted ball will have a difficult time rolling foul. The grass both in the infield and in the outfield can be kept mowed closely or allowed to grow, depending upon whether the home team thinks it more or less advantageous to its cause to slow up balls hit on the ground or help speed them on their way.

The coming of artificial "grass," of course, has severely limited the skills and enterprise of groundskeepers in this respect. It has also wrought significant changes in the way the game is played. The potentiality for freak hops on routine ground balls has been all but eliminated, to the gratification of the infielders. However, a ball hit on artificial turf moves faster and bounces higher, and its chances of skidding through gaps in the infield for base hits has been greatly increased. It used to be that the most advantageous build for a shortstop was to be lean and lanky, along the lines of a Marty Marion or a Roy McMillan; today the ability to stretch out is less important than to be able to

make sudden, swift movements, because a hard-hit ground ball will fly off an artificial infield surface with bewildering rapidity. Thus the top shortstop in the majors today, Ozzie Smith of the Cardinals, is renowned for the incredible quickness of his reflexes.

Whether a baseball diamond's surface be natural or artificial, however, the standards of field maintenance nowadays are far higher than back in the earlier years of the century. The infield surface is much truer, with less opportunity for ground balls to take erratic bounces. The ball may come off the turf faster, but its path will be more predictable. Outfielders may have to play further back on line drives because when the ball hits the surface it may otherwise bound over their heads, but the chances of the ball striking a pothole or a rock and making a sudden 45-degree swerve off its supposed trajectory are minimized — unless, of course, the ball happens to land squarely upon one of the seams in the artificial carpet, in which case anything can happen.

It is highly unlikely nowadays that there will be a repetition of the events that transpired at Griffith Stadium in Washington, D.C., in the seventh game of the 1924 World Series between the Senators and the New York Giants. With the Series tied at three games apiece, the Giants were leading by 3-1 in the eighth inning. Then, with baserunners on second and third, manager Bucky Harris of the Senators hit a routine grounder at the New York shortstop, Freddie Lindstrom. The ball struck a pebble, bounded high over Lindstrom's head, and both runs crossed, tying the score.

No runs were scored in the ninth, and the game went into extra innings. In the twelfth inning, with one man out, Washington catcher Muddy Ruel lofted a fly ball in foul territory behind the plate. Hank Gowdy, the Giants' catcher, who in order to follow the ball's flight had removed his mask and dropped it to the ground, stumbled on it and missed the ball. Given renewed life, Ruel promptly doubled down the third base line. The Senator's great pitcher, Walter Johnson, who had come in in relief in the ninth inning, hit a ball at shortstop Stony Jackson, who bobbled it, sending Ruel to third with the potential winning run.

At that point the Washington leadoff batter, center-fielder Earl McNeely, hit an easy ground ball at Lindstrom. Again, however, the ball struck a pebble and went sailing over Lindstrom's head. Ruel came in to score, and Walter Johnson, at the age of 36 and after eighteen years in the majors, finally won a World Series game and the Senators a championship.

Whether the Senators voted a share of the winner's money to the Griffith Stadium grounds-keeper is not known. There were those, however, who felt that the Almighty himself had intervened on behalf of Johnson, who during all the years of his long and distinguished career on the Washington Senators had toiled on behalf of teams that were otherwise made up of mostly second-rate players. As Jack Bentley of the Giants, the losing pitcher in the game, said, "Walter Johnson is such a lovable character that the Good Lord didn't want to see him get beat again."

III

IN THE CLUBHOUSE

Lockers, Busch Stadium, 1986

Vida Blue, Dodger Stadium, 1986

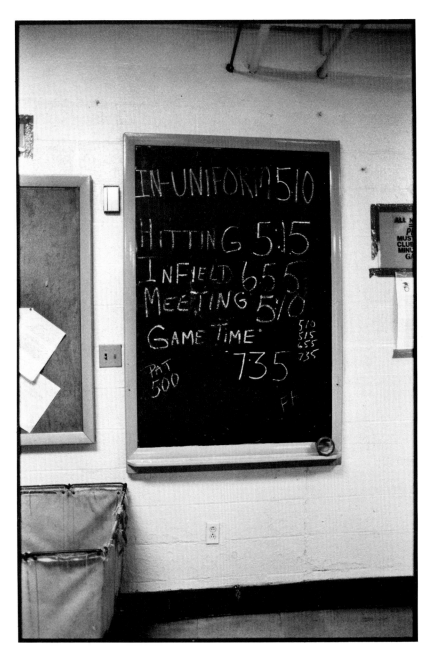

Blackboard, Memorial Stadium, 1986

San Francisco Giants, Dodger Stadium, 1986

*S*o much is going on in the hours before a game —
examinations, rehabilitation, prescriptions, coach-
ing. And all of it to a backdrop of shuffling cards,
blaring stereos, chattering players and coarse words
between clubhouse attendants and players.

George Vecsey, columnist

Chris Brown and Giants, Dodger Stadium, 1986

*I like to and most of the guys like coming out early
to get that closeness you have with your teammates.
It gets you in a ballgame type atmosphere that you
need to have. During the winter, you want to get back
there, you want to get that relationship going again.*
                                        Roger McDowell

Juan Samuel, Veterans Stadium, 1986

Von Hayes, Veterans Stadium, 1986

Cubs playing cards, Wrigley Field, 1986

Especially on the road, some of us go to the ballpark six or seven hours before the game. You're gone away from your home, you're away from your family, you really don't have that much to do. After a while the hotel rooms get smaller and smaller and smaller. Most of us would rather spend our time at the ballpark with the friends that we have to play cards, to read, to talk about baseball, to do something. It's the feeling of loneliness on the road why a lot of guys come to the ballpark early.

Ron Guidry

Eddie Murray, playing video game, Memorial Stadium, 1986

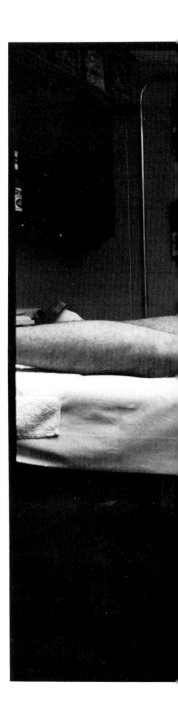

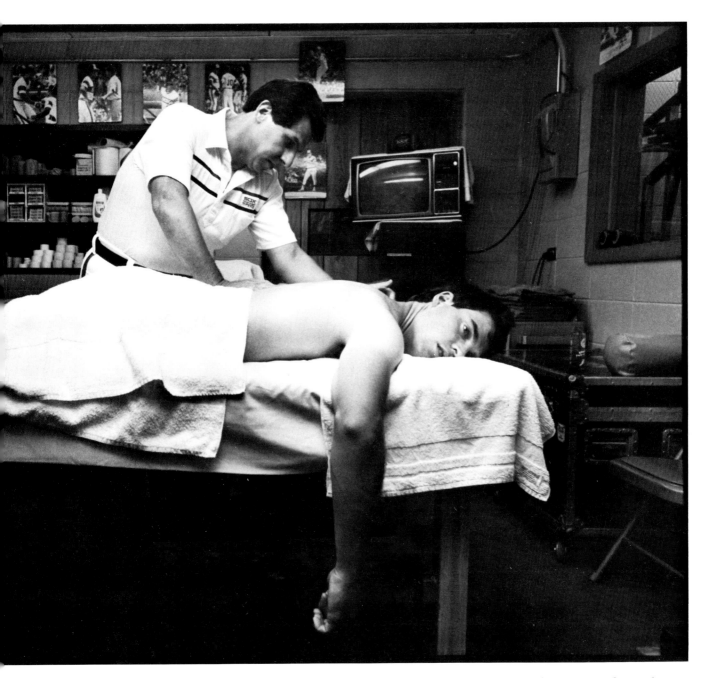

Trainer Herb Schneider and Joel Skinner, Comiskey Park, 1986

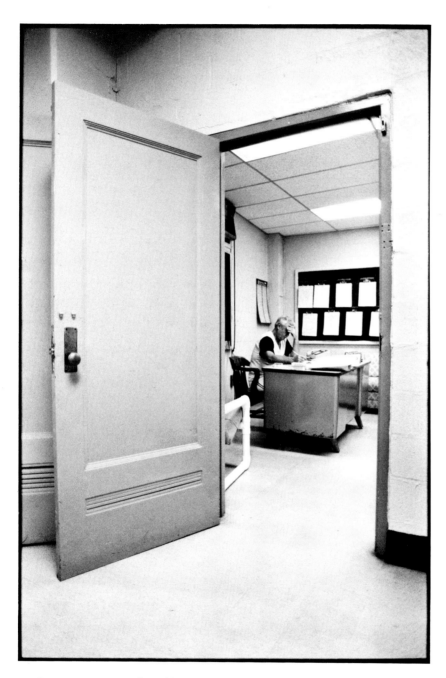

Earl Weaver, Memorial Stadium, 1986

Whitey Herzog and reporter, Busch Stadium, 1986

Keith Hernandez and visitor, Shea Stadium, 1986

*I looked around at their faces: they were so familiar
and, at the same time, closed utterly to the outside.
They knew instinctively how to keep their privacy.
They had perfected remoteness in intimacy.*
                                                Richard Grossinger, writer

Gary Carter and reporter, Shea Stadium, 1986

In their brief season, they sit for a thousand after-noons in front of their lockers, pull on archaic stockings, set their knickers at the height they affect, and josh and tease their teammates. Tony the trainer measures a tender elbow, tapes an ankle. Then the citizens saunter without urgency onto the field, gloves under arms, and pick up a ball.

Donald Hall

St. Louis Cardinals in Sunday prayer, Busch Stadium, 1986

IV

TAKING THE FIELD

Steve Garvey, San Diego-Jack Murphy Stadium, 1986

At the batrack, Anaheim Stadium, 1986

Batting cage, County Stadium, 1986

Batting cage, Tiger Stadium, 1986

Batting practice pitcher, Yankee Stadium, 1987

Graig Nettles, Yankee Stadium, 1979

Baltimore Orioles, Fenway Park, 1986

The hours that we have for batting practice before each game is a time to get yourself ready for the game. Stretching, throwing, getting your muscles ready. You try to feel good in batting practice and carry it over to the ballgame. It's done day in and day out. It's a routine.

                                    Rick Cerone

Ed Whitson warms up as Galen Cisco looks on, San Diego-Jack Murphy Stadium, 1986

Chris Speier, Wrigley Field, 1986

As your mind must be concentrated when you face an opponent, so, too, your practice must include this mental effort.

Sadaharu Oh

Don Mattingly, Comiskey Park, 1986

Dale Murphy, Atlanta-Fulton County Stadium, 1986

Red Sox pitchers, Fenway Park, 1986

It is the best of all games for me. It frequently escapes from the pattern of sport and assumes the form of a virile ballet. It is purer than any dance because the actions of the players are not governed by music or crowded into a formula by a director. The movement is natural and unrehearsed and controlled only by the unexpected flight of the ball.

Jimmy Cannon

New York Mets before the game, Shea Stadium, 1986

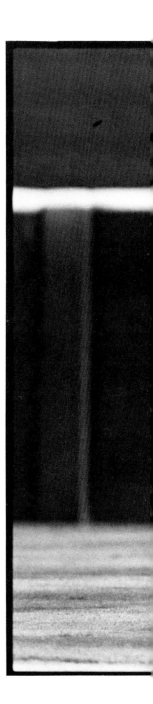

Gene Tenace hitting fungoes, San Diego-Jack Murphy Stadium, 1986

Ozzie Smith, San Diego-Jack Murphy Stadium, 1986

Dickie Thon, San Diego-Jack Murphy Stadium, 1986

Phillie outfielder shagging flies, Veterans Stadium, 1986

George Brett, Royals Stadium, World Series, 1985

San Francisco Giants, Dodger Stadium, 1986

*E*veryone is relaxed and slightly self-conscious,
repeating the motions that became rote before they
were ten.

Donald Hall

Carl Yastrzemski, Yankee Stadium, 1980

Montreal Expos, Wrigley Field, 1986

More than any other games, baseball gives its players space — both physical and emotional — in which to define themselves.

John Eskow, writer

Cardinal pitchers, Busch Stadium, 1986

Meanwhile, as the grounds crew is working over the diamond and the grandstands are beginning to fill up, the players on both the home and visiting teams are out of sight in the locker room and clubhouse, thinking about the game to come, preparing for it.

Almost always there will be a team meeting, primarily in order to go over the opposing team's lineup and decide how the individual batters are to be handled. There are extensive records available to indicate just what kinds of pitches were thrown to batters in previous games, and what was done to them. If during a game you look down into the dugout of either team you will see someone, usually the next day's starting pitcher, keeping a chart on which is recorded each pitch made to opposing batters, what kind it was, where it was thrown, and what the batter did with it.

No two pitchers pitch exactly the same way, and what works for one may not work for the other. Still, it can be useful to know that a particular batter hit two fastballs thrown high and away for base hits, but when thrown a fastball high and well outside the strike zone and then given a curveball down and inside, swung and missed. Chances are that any fastball he will see will be up and far outside, and will be followed by a curve thrown inside and at the knees.

Not only pitchers but infielders and outfielders can make good use of knowledge of a batter's hitting habits. If with a runner on first base a left-handed batter is to be pitched tight, the chances of his being able to pull the ball will be increased, since he will be swinging in on the ball rather than out at it. The second baseman, there-fore, will probably want to station himself deep and shaded toward first base, while the shortstop will play closer to second base to handle balls hit up the middle and to take the throw from the catcher if the runner breaks for second base. The center fielder will play a few steps closer toward right field, while the right fielder will move toward the foul line and play deeper. And so on.

Prior knowledge of a batter's preferences and his speed in getting down to first base can sometimes make a considerable difference. In the 1933 World Series between the New York Giants and the Washington Senators, New York had taken a two-to-one advantage in games, and in the top of the eleventh inning of the fourth game had broken a tie and scored the go-ahead run. The Giants' ace pitcher, Carl Hubbell, now had only to shut down the Senators in their half of the eleventh. Washington, however, was able to get baserunners on second and third with only one out. The next Washington batter, catcher Luke Sewell, had already collected two hits off Hubbell that day, so the Giants decided to put him on first base, loading the bases and setting up a potential double play.

At that juncture Manager Joe Cronin of Washington called upon a pinch hitter, Cliff Bolton, a young catcher up from Chattanooga of the Southern Association. None of the Giants on the field, including player-manager Bill Terry at first base, had any information on how to pitch to Bolton. Should Hubbell go all-out for a strikeout, or would it be a better idea to give Bolton something that he would be likely to hit on the ground?

Charlie Dressen, a Giant player-coach, had seen the young catcher in action in Southern Association play, so he called time and ran out on the field. Bolton, he reported, was a good hitter, but very slow afoot. So Hubbell pitched Bolton low and away, Bolton rapped a double-play ball to the shortstop, and the Giants won. Without Dressen's timely information Bolton might have been given a pitch that he could have pulled over third base or shortstop into left field, and the tying and winning runs might have scored.

Not all pitchers are able to make use of information about a batter's strengths and weaknesses. Not all pitchers *want* to make use of it. A pitcher with an overpowering fastball, for example, may very well disdain to set up a batter by throwing at his weaknesses. Convinced that he can fire his fastball by any hitter, no matter how skilled, he will simply reach back and throw his heater, as the fastball is often called, past the batter.

Consider, therefore, the plight of the late Frankie Frisch as manager of the St. Louis Cardinals in 1934. Frisch had learned his baseball under John McGraw, of the old Giants, and when the Little Napoleon of the Polo Grounds gave orders to his players he wanted them obeyed. Before each game McGraw usually instructed his pitchers and catchers on how they were to pitch to various batters, and the Giant infielders and outfielders were told where they were to play. McGraw

was also in the habit of giving pre-game instruction to his own hitters as to what they were expected to do at the plate. On one occasion he flashed a bunt sign, but the batter, seeing a pitch coming in just where he likes it, chose instead to swing away, and drove it over the fence for a home run. After circling the bases he returned triumphantly to the dugout, only to be fined $100 by McGraw for disobeying orders.

Such was the tutelage under which Frank Frisch learned his trade. But when Frisch became manager of the Cardinals in 1934, he soon found that McGraw's managerial style of giving detailed instructions to pitchers, fielders, and batters would not always work, in particular with his star right-handed pitcher Dizzy Dean. On one occasion Frisch was going over the opposing hitters with his team before a game, when Dean rose to his feet. "Oh hell, why waste all this time talking about pitching?" he informed Frisch. "There's only one way to pitch. Just go out there and blow 'em down."

In truth Dean was capable of doing exactly that, and Frisch knew it. "If you can blow 'em down," he told Joe Williams of the *World-Telegram,* "it is not important to know whether to keep the ball high or low, inside or out. Dizzy can blow 'em down. Besides his natural power he has an instinct for pitching wisely."

What works for a Dean, a Lefty Grove, a Bob Feller, or a Roger Clemens, however, will not suffice for most journeyman pitchers, who must get batters out without the extraordinary physical equipment that the game's star pitchers can bring to the job. The average pitcher in the major leagues needs all the information he can get on opposing hitters.

When attempting to hold strategy meetings Frank Frisch also had his troubles with the irrepressible John Leonard Martin, known as Pepper. On one occasion, as reported by Curt Smith in his biography of Dizzy Dean, the Cardinal manager was meeting with his players before game time, and was industriously reviewing the batting strengths and weaknesses of that day's opponents. As the meeting proceeded, Frisch talked on and on, as was his wont. Then Martin spoke up.

"Frank, can I ask you a question?"

"Yeah, what?"

"Frankie, I was just wondering if I ought to paint my midget auto racer red with white wheels or white with red wheels?"

Depending on the personnel involved, a pre-game meeting can be no more than a hollow ritual. Once when Gabby Street was manager the Cardinals were discussing the batting habits of the Chicago Cubs preparatory to engaging them in combat. The designated St. Louis pitcher of the day was Flint Rhem, a decent pitcher who was notably fond of the bottle. (It was Rhem who in 1931 was scheduled to pitch against the Giants in New York, but disappeared for two days. When eventually he showed up for duty, considerably·the worse for wear, he reported that two gunmen had kidnapped him, escorted him over to a speakeasy in New Jersey, and then with drawn pistols had forced him to drink so much whiskey that he had

been unable to escape and make his way back to the Cardinals' hotel in Manhattan.)

Street went down the Chicago lineup: Billy Herman, Woody English, Kiki Cuyler, Riggs Stephenson, Johnny Moore, etc., on through to the pitcher of the day. The preferences and the weaknesses of each batter were described and discussed, and Rhem then explained how he intended to pitch to them. "I'll ace 'em, and then I'll deuce 'em," he responded invariably. When the skull session was completed, Street was forced to face the fact that Rhem had absorbed precisely nothing of what had been said, and that whoever the Chicago batter might be, the Cardinals' starting pitcher would pitch him exactly the same: first a fastball, then a curve, and beyond that with no planned strategy whatever.

Before Babe Ruth became the greatest home run hitter ever, as all students of the game know, he was one of the top left-handed pitchers of his day for the then-mighty Boston Red Sox. A smart pitcher, able to exploit weaknesses in opposing batters, Ruth was not inclined even so to spend excessive amounts of time concentrating on what was being said in pre-game meetings.

As manager of the Red Sox in 1918, Ed Barrow assigned Ruth the task of facing the Chicago Cubs in the first game of the 1918 World Series. In the pre-game strategy meeting he warned Ruth that when pitching to the Cubs he should take special pains not to allow Les Mann, the Chicago left fielder, to get a toehold when at bat. Mann, he explained, was a right-handed hitter and could be very rough on left-handed pitching. "Watch out for this fellow Mann," he told Ruth. "Don't let up on him. Don't ever let him dig in at the plate."

"Don't worry," Ruth said, "I'll get him."

As Robert Creamer relates in his biography of Ruth, Les Mann was a short and stocky individual. Max Flack, the Chicago right fielder, was also short of stature, though not nearly so chunky as Mann. Moreover, Flack batted left-handed, not right-handed.

In the first inning Flack led off for the Cubs. Ruth studied him closely, then brushed him back from the plate twice and got him on a called third strike with a fastball outside. As for Mann, when he came up he singled sharply.

In the third inning Flack got a hit, so when he came to bat again two innings later Ruth hit him atop the head with a fastball. Fortunately Flack was unhurt and took his base. When the inning was over Ruth returned to the dugout and sat down next to Barrow. "Well, I guess I took care of that guy Mann for you," he told his manager. He had been throwing at the wrong batter. So much for pre-game strategy.

Pitching has been described by baseball men as constituting anywhere from 65 to 80 percent of the game. The high valuation is not difficult to understand; one need only think of what a really good pitcher can do to silence even the best-hitting of ball clubs. The most obvious instance of this is the World Series of 1960, when Casey Stengel's last New York Yankee team outhit the Pittsburgh Pirates .338 to .256, scored 55 runs to the Pirates' 27, with ten homers to Pittsburgh's four. Yet Danny

Murtaugh's Pirates took the Series four games to three, mainly because when right-hander Vern Law and lefty Harvey Haddix were pitching, they were able to contain the Yankee attack. Thirty-eight of New York's 55 runs were scored in the three games won by the Yankees, all by top-heavy scores. In four other games Law and Haddix kept the score low, and the Pittsburgh attack generated the runs necessary to win.

The great "dynasties" of baseball history have usually had at least two top-drawer pitchers — "stoppers" who could be counted on to bring a halt to any losing streaks their teams ran into. Both of Connie Mack's championship teams in Philadelphia were anchored by magnificent pitching — Chief Bender, Eddie Plank, and Jack Coombs for the Athletics of the early 1910s, Lefty Grove, George Earnshaw, and Rube Walberg for the 1929-1931 club. Power hitting has always been considered the forte of the New York Yankees over the years, and rightly so, but the Murderers' Row of the 1920s had a championship pitching staff, too, in Waite Hoyt, Herb Pennock, Bob Shawkey, Wilcy Moore, and George Pipgras, while the Bronx Bombers of the 1930s had a pair of superb "stoppers" in Red Ruffing and Lefty Gomez, and Johnny Murphy in relief. Casey Stengel's clubs in the late 1940s and 1950s had Vic Raschi, Allie Reynolds, and Ed Lopat, and later Whitey Ford and Bob Turley.

The Brooklyn teams that were constantly in contention during the 1940s and 1950s were staffed at the outset with Whitlow Wyatt, Kirby Higbe, and Hugh Casey, then Don Newcombe, Carl Erskine, Ralph Branca, Johnny Podres, and Ed Roebuck, while the succeeding Los Angeles dynasty of the 1960s depended absolutely upon the matchless combination of Sandy Koufax and Don Drysdale, as well as Podres and Ron Perranoski.

The reign of the Oakland A's of the 1960s lasted for just as long as Jim Hunter, Ken Holtzman, Blue Moon Odom, and Rollie Fingers were content to pitch for a team owned by the mercurial and erratic Charlie Finley. The Baltimore Orioles of the same period had Jim Palmer, Dave McNally, Wally Bunker, and Mike Cuellar.

The only two "great" teams of baseball history (by which is meant teams that consistently won pennants and World Series over a period of some years) that were not blessed with top-line pitching staffs were the New York Giants of the early 1920s and the Big Red Machine of Cincinnati during the middle 1970s. John McGraw's club finished atop the National League four years in a row, from 1921 through 1924, and twice won the World Series, without any really dominant pitchers. What McGraw did have, however, was more-than-competent spot pitching. Somebody was always ready when needed, and he was able to move an assortment of good pitchers in and out of games. It was a pitching staff without standouts; during four championship years the Giants only had one twenty-game winner, Art Nehf in 1921. (Contrast that with the pennant-winning Baltimore Orioles, with three twenty-game winners in 1971 and four in 1972.)

As for Sparky Anderson's powerhouse clubs of the 1970s, they won because their manager used tactics similar to those of McGraw in the 1920s. Anderson earned the nickname of Captain Hook for the alacrity with which he headed out to the mount to remove starting pitchers and summon relievers. More so than any other major league manager it was Sparky who faced up to the logic of the changing role of the relief pitcher in the game. There was no inherent virtue, he realized, in a pitcher's working a complete game, provided that good pitching was on call in the bullpen. So again and again he signalled for Pedro Borbon and Clay Carroll, and in 1975 and 1976 Rawly Eastwick and Will McEnaney, to come into close games and take over.

Throughout the period from 1972 through 1976, the Reds were without a single twenty-game winner. Like McGraw, Anderson made excellent use of middle relievers, in effect maintaining a corps of sometime-starters, sometime-relievers whose job was to keep the score down long enough for the short relief to take over. To be sure, part of the reason why it worked so well was that the Reds had a tremendous hitting team, with no weak spots whatever in the batting order, so that airtight pitching was not usually required. But as we have seen, even the heaviest hitting of ball clubs can be thoroughly negated by first-rate pitching, and if the Big Red Machine hadn't been able to deliver more than merely competent pitching, in whatever combinations, all that the Messrs. Pete Rose, Johnny Bench, George Foster, Tony Perez, Dave Concepcion, Joe Morgan, Ken Griffey, etc., were able to do at bat would not have produced those four divisional titles, three National League pennants, and two world championships in five seasons for Sparky Anderson's mighty Cincinnatians.

There is no set number of throws required to get a pitcher ready to open a ball game. In chilly weather it will take longer than on midsummer days and evenings, but different pitchers have different routines. Most pitchers like to begin while close to the catcher, lobbing a half-dozen or more throws and then gradually stepping back until they are standing on the slab at the regulation sixty feet, six inches away from the plate. Other pitchers, such as Sudden Sam McDowell, who won 141 major league games between 1961 and 1974, prefer to move well behind the slab until they are as far as eighty feet away. Most pitchers do this so that they can make long, loose throws to stretch their arm muscles. Only then will they set up at the regulation distance and begin pitching rather than merely throwing the ball. McDowell, who did most things differently during his career, began throwing hard on his first pitch.

The usual routine is to throw fastballs, gradually increasing the velocity until the pitcher is approaching something close to game speed, and then to start tossing breaking balls, at first slowly and with only enough of a turn of the wrist to give the ball a spinning motion, and then after the wrist muscles have been thoroughly loosened to begin imparting a definite snap to the wrist as it turns over. Throwing too rapidly too soon, and snapping off curves before the arm is thoroughly tuned up, is a good way to risk pulling a muscle and damaging the arm.

To throw a baseball any way other than underhanded, or straight over the top without any turning of the hand and wrist, is said to be fundamentally an unnatural motion; the human biceps and tendons are not designed to throw a baseball while bending the elbow and snapping the wrist. Perhaps the hardest pitch of all on the arm is the screwball, which is thrown either overhand or with a three-quarter motion. The pitcher grips the ball much like the fastball, but he cocks his wrist back and turns it slightly outward, rather than inward as with a normal curveball. As he brings the ball forward he turns his wrist and hand over sharply, so that instead of the palm of his hand facing down, as with the fastball, it ends up turned in toward his body.

To do this while also bringing the arm over at full strength places a tremendous strain on the elbow and the muscles of the forearm, because in effect they are being opposed to the movement of the full arm and shoulder. A screwball cannot be made to break very much, but it doesn't have to bend in its flight more than a few inches; the motion and delivery of the pitch resemble that of a fastball so closely that the batter expects the ball to come in high and hard. When at the last moment it takes a slight dip or bend, it is quite enough to cause the batter to miss it entirely or hit it only a glancing blow.

For some reason, most of the successful screwball pitchers have been left-handers, although the first great practitioner of the pitch, Christy Mathewson, threw right-handed. Mathewson called the pitch a Fadeway — which is to say, a seemingly straight pitch that at the last instant faded away from the batter. It was not really Mathewson's "bread and butter" pitch; he used it only sparingly, in key situations. In his book *Pitching In a Pinch*, he declared that "it takes so much out of my arm. It is a very hard ball to deliver. Pitching it ten or twelve times in a game kills my arm, so I save it for the pinches."

It was precisely the notion that throwing the screwball was certain to cause arm damage that caused the Detroit Tigers to give up on one of the finest of all left-handed pitchers, Carl Hubbell. Detroit had owned Hubbell's contract and had brought him to training camp on two occasions, once when Ty Cobb was manager and again under George Moriarty, and had written him off as a poor investment.

The story, as told by the late Frank Graham in his book *The New York Giants,* goes that Dick Kinsella, who scouted for John McGraw and the Giants, went down to Houston, Texas, as a delegate from Illinois to the 1928 Democratic Party convention, and decided to skip an afternoon session in favor of a Texas League game between the Beaumont Oilers and the Houston Buffs. When he saw Hubbell on the mound for Beaumont he forgot all about Al Smith and presidential politics. Making discreet inquiries he learned that although Beaumont had a working agreement with Detroit, Hubbell had been released outright to them. He then got hold of John McGraw in New York.

The Giant skipper had been Christy Mathewson's manager, and saw nothing wrong with signing a screwball pitcher. So Kinsella spent several weeks trailing Beaumont around the circuit, then called McGraw again and recommended his purchase. Hubbell, who had already won a dozen games for the Oilers that summer, departed forthwith for the Polo Grounds, and picked up ten additional victories for the Giants before the 1928 season was done.

It was not Hubbell's habit to limit himself to only a few screwball pitches per game; he threw it so regularly and often that his left arm became permanently canted inward. In Hubbell's heyday many a young Giant fan went around with his pitching arm turned in, in emulation of the Master. In 1938 the pitch did finally bring Hubbell arm trouble, and he was forced to undergo an operation to have bone chips removed from his elbow, but not before he had pitched the Giants to three National League pennants and registered five straight twenty-game seasons between 1933 and 1937. In 1933, when Hubbell opened the World Series with a five-hit, 4-2 victory over the Washington Senators, striking out ten batters, the umpire calling the balls and strikes was George Moriarty.

Tug McGraw used a screwball to good effect as a relief pitcher during the 1970s and early 1980s for the Mets and the Phillies, Tom Brewer threw it for the Red Sox, and Luis Arroyo for the Yankees. But the top screwball pitcher since Hubbell's days is probably Fernando Valenzuela of the present-day Dodgers. When the stocky 20-year-old left-hander made his spectacular entry onto the Los Angeles scene in the strike-divided split season of 1981, winning both the Cy Young and Rookie of the Year awards, Hubbell observed him in action and declared that what made Fernando's screwball so effective was that he threw it overhand, just as he himself had done. Also, like Hubbell, Valenzuela throws the pitch frequently, and in seven subsequent seasons has shown no sign of arm trouble.

It has been said that the advent of the slider as a major pitch in the game is what more than any other single factor is responsible for the general falling off of batting averages from the late 1940s onward. It too is thrown like the fastball, and curves only slightly, but because the batter believes until the last moment that it *is* a fastball, only to have it veer off course, the slight break and reduced velocity can be tremendously effective.

Unlike the screwball, the slider is thrown with very little wrist turn, but unlike the fastball it is gripped across the seams, with the index and middle fingers positioned somewhat to the side rather than across the top. When the pitcher brings his hand down the fingers pull down on the seam, producing sufficient lateral spin to make it break slightly. If a slider is thrown properly, it is a greatly deceptive weapon, but it is a hard pitch to learn. A touch too much wrist action and the pitch is slowed up until it is no more than a gentle curve that can be hit hard and far. Too little wrist action and it is a fastball without full zip, beloved by good batters.

Ted Williams, who may have been the greatest hitter ever, insisted that the slider was the most difficult pitch to hit in the entire baseball repertoire. But Martin Quigley, in his splendid history of the curveball, *The Crooked Pitch,* quotes Clyde McCullough, longtime Chicago Cub catcher, as saying that although if thrown well "it's a hell of a pitch," he had seen more home runs hit off sliders than any other pitch.

The master of the slider was Steve Carlton, lately come upon evil seasons but in his prime — a prime that extended for more than a decade — the best left-hander of his era. Along with his slider went a pretty good fastball and a better than good curve. In 22 years in the majors Carlton won more than 330 games and struck out more than four thousand batters.

"Without the deception of the curveball," Quigley writes in *The Crooked Pitch,* "baseball would have become just another sport for young men of premium size and strength." He calls it "The Great Equalizer," because finesse in throwing it can make a pint-sized pitcher as dangerous as any behemoth with a high hard one. Joe McCarthy, manager of the powerful Yankee clubs of the 1930s, always insisted that there were *no* really good curveball hitters. There is little doubt that the ability to hit a curveball with reasonable effectiveness is what distinguishes major league from minor league hitters. Even in the high minors it is possible for a batter to lay off the curveball and swing at fastballs only, but in the major leagues too many pitchers can consistently throw the curve for strikes, and batters who cannot defend against it will not be around for very long.

For predominantly fastball pitchers such as Dwight Gooden, Roger Clemens, Nolan Ryan, Tom Seaver, Bob Feller, Robin Roberts, Lefty

Grove, and others, the function of the curveball was and is to keep hitters honest. It is thrown just enough so that a batter cannot dig in and begin timing the fastball. Occasionally a young pitcher like Feller or Ryan comes along with such blazing speed that at first even the best major league batters cannot lay the bat on him. But after a time the good hitters become sufficiently accustomed to the young pitcher's fastball to be able to set themselves at the plate and time their swings. Or let the young fireballer become only a bit older and begin to lose a little of his speed — a few inches off his fastball, as they say — and the base hits commence to multiply.

What Feller and Ryan and other top pitchers who came into the majors throwing nothing but smoke were able to do was to develop a decent curveball and learn how to change speeds effectively. No longer could opposing batters count on getting a diet consisting exclusively of fastballs. The high hard pitch could therefore continue to be thrown with maximum effectiveness.

The only great pitcher who is said never to have developed even a moderately effective curve was Walter Johnson. Throughout his 20-year career with the Senators, Johnson apparently stuck to the fastball almost exclusively. The occasional curve he is described as having thrown he apparently threw overhand instead of his usual sidearm style. The Big Train, as he was called, was not however an orthodox fastball pitcher. Contemporary photographs indicate that he possessed big hands and almost abnormally long arms, and that unlike almost all other fastball virtuosi he threw from the side, not down and in.

Davy Jones described Johnson's pitching motion to Lawrence Ritter, in *The Glory of Their Times,* this way: "He had those long arms, absolutely the longest arms I ever saw. They were like whips, that's what they were. He'd just *whip* that ball in there." Sam Crawford, a better hitter than Jones, told Ritter than Johnson's pitching reminded him of "one of those compressed-air pitching machines . . . it comes in so fast that when it goes by it *swooshes.* . . . He had such an easy motion it looked like he was just playing catch. That's what threw you off. He threw so nice and easy — and then *swoosh,* and it was by you!"

What with the elongated arms, the elongated fingers, the sidearm "buggy whip" delivery, the easy motion, and the sudden velocity, characteristics to which numerous batters who faced him all refer, it sounds very much as if Johnson's wrist action must have played an important role in his pitching. Ozzie Bluege described it to Donald Honig this way: "He used to sort of slip that thing up there sidearm, almost underhand, and you'd think that ball was going to come right at you, and you'd back off and swipe at it, but it was right over the plate. The ball would rise; it would swoosh and rise."

Enough batters have testified to the fact that they could actually hear Johnson's fastball as it came in to make it seem likely that more than a little spin was being imparted as it left the pitcher's hands. The same phenomenon has been reported for Sandy Koufax's tremendously fast curveball.

The only thing that could possibly cause the "swooshing" sound would be the rapidly-spinning seams. Photographs of Johnson showing his pitching arm and hand reveal that at the completion of his delivery the palm faced down, and since he was a sidearmer this means that as he was releasing the ball he was in the habit of turning his wrist over. It sounds, therefore, as if Johnson's famed swooshing "fastball" may not have been a straight fastball after all, but something like a sinker, a screwball without the sharp elbow-wrenching, muscle-jerking twist, with the fingers imparting spin as the ball was released, but thrown sidearm so that when it veered it broke downward. Everyone who has described it has insisted that Johnson's fastball was *live;* it did not come in on a flat trajectory, but *moved.* So I wonder whether it is in fact true that in his heyday the great Walter Johnson threw nothing but a straight fastball to all batters. He just might have been coming in sidearm with something resembling a slider or sinker!

By the time that the field is ready for a ball game to begin, both starting pitchers have completed their warm-ups, although the visiting club's pitcher may prefer to work at a more leisurely pace and to complete his preparations down by the bullpen area while his team is batting. Very rare indeed is the pitcher who like the great Grover Cleveland Alexander can get by with no more than a few minutes of limbering up. When it was time to get ready Alexander would throw a dozen or so pitches, none of them very hard, and thereaf-

ter was prepared to face the opposing batters. Tall and with short stubby fingers, Alexander threw a "heavy" ball — a pitch with very little movement of the seams that when it smacked into the catcher's mitt seemed almost to burn its way through the leather padding. By the mid-1920s, when he was in his late thirties and early forties, he had made up for the gradual loss of speed by achieving an incredible, pinpoint accuracy on his pitches. Occasionally he threw a screwball that broke in on right-handed batters, and he changed speeds constantly.

Some idea of the impact that the use of short relief pitching has had on the game can be seen by looking at Alexander's complete games totals in 1927, when he was forty years old but won 21 and lost 11 games for the St. Louis Cardinals. He was the starting pitcher in 30 games and he completed 22! And that figure was far from the best in the major leagues that year; three other National League pitchers completed 25 games apiece, while Ted Lyons of the Chicago White Sox started 34 ball games and finished all but 4! (In the "dead ball" era before World War I the difference was even more pronounced; in his rookie season of 1915, for example, when Alexander won 31 games for the Philadelphia Phillies, he started 42 ballgames and completed all but 6!)

Before the advent of the fulltime relief pitcher, a good starting pitcher actively and sometimes vociferously resented being removed from a game before it was over. The most celebrated demonstration of such resentment, of course, was that staged by Walter "Boom Boom" Beck of the Dodgers in the early 1930s, who when manager Casey Stengel evicted him from the game became so enraged that he threw the ball all the way to the right-field fence on the fly in Philadelphia's Baker Bowl. The sudden crash of baseball against fence so startled right-fielder Hack Wilson, who was engaged in a booze-scented reverie while awaiting resumption of the game, that he wheeled, fielded the ball off the wall, and threw a perfect strike to second base to hold the "runner" to a single. But most starting pitchers of the pre-Hoyt Wilhelm era deemed themselves insulted and injured if removed from a ballgame without what they considered to be sufficient cause. They were paid, they believed, to pitch all nine innings of the game, and more if the game required extra innings.

It is not, of course, true that the institution of the full-time relief pitcher is entirely a phenomenon of the modern game. Firpo Marberry, of the Washington Senators, was probably the first pitcher to build a reputation principally on finishing rather than starting games; in 1925 he appeared in 55 games, never as a starter, and by today's measurements would have had 15 saves. The New York Yankees used Wilcy Moore almost exclusively as a reliever during their world championship seasons of 1927 and 1928. Right-hander Johnny Murphy was renowned during the Yankees' great years of the late 1930s and early 1940s for coming to the relief of the Bronx Bombers' starting pitchers, and particularly of Lefty Gomez, who once told an interviewer that he owed his success as a major league pitcher to clean living, prayer, and Johnny Murphy's arm.

Not until the 1940s, however, did the number of games that relief pitchers work begin significantly rising. In 1943 the last-place New York Giants' Ace Adams established a new record when he appeared in 70 of his team's 156 games, only three times as the starting pitcher. The year following, Joe Heving of Cleveland got into 83 games, while Adams increased his total to 85.

But the first *winning* ball team to employ a pitcher not merely to replace inadequate starting pitching when needed, but to come into games in late innings even though the starter was still doing a creditable job, in order to safeguard victories, was the 1947 Dodgers. In that season Hugh Casey entered 46 ball games, most of them close contests, pitched a total of only 77 innings, won 10, lost only 4, and chalked up 18 saves. Casey was thus the first true modern short relief specialist who did that and only that for a living. That same season, however, the world champion Yankees used Joe Page in almost the same way, and two years later Page set a record for saves (although "saves" as such were not made part of the official records until the late 1960s) with 27.

It was Jim Konstanty of the Phillies who, more than any other pitcher, was responsible for the rise of the relief specialist to full star status. A lanky right-hander who had been in organized baseball for ten years without attracting much attention, Konstanty clearly meant the difference to the Philadelphia "Whiz Kids" in the National League pennant race. No kid himself — he was 33 years old — Konstanty had a fantastic season. Until he joined the Phillies he had always been a starting pitcher, but manager Eddie Sawyer decided to use him entirely in relief. Appearing in 74 games in 1950, he won 16 of them and had 22 saves. On the strength of his performance out of the bullpen Konstanty was chosen the National League's Most Valuable Player for the 1950 season, the first time that the award had ever gone to a relief pitcher.

The MVP award to Konstanty made it official: where in earlier years a reliever was a pitcher who wasn't good enough to make it into the regular pitching rotation, now he was a fulltime specialist in closing out games, possessing the particular kinds of skills that enabled him to do that job. It had taken a half-century and more for major league baseball to realize the full value of having a fresh pitcher to come in toward the end of a close ball game, just when the starter might be beginning to tire, ready and able to go at full speed for two or three innings. Today all major league clubs have designated middle relief pitchers and "closers." Indeed, some teams will often have two such late relief specialists, a right-hander and a left-hander, and no team can win the big games without one such performer.

What the absence of the late reliever can mean was vividly demonstrated in the 1982 World Series, when the St. Louis Cardinals came back from a deficit of three games to two to defeat the Milwaukee Brewers. Both clubs had first-rate relievers, Bruce Sutter for St. Louis and Rollie Fingers for Milwaukee. But Fingers, who had saved 29 regular season games for the Brewers, had injured his arm shortly before the close of the season, and although his team was able to outlast the California Angels in the divisional playoffs, not having him available

to close out games during the Series proved to be fatal.

Twice the Brewers lost because their pitchers were unable to protect late-inning leads. In the final game Milwaukee went into the bottom of the sixth inning leading 3-1, only to have the Cardinals put runners at second and third with one out. Had Fingers been healthy, Manager Harvey Kuenn would then and there have summoned him to stop the Cardinal rally. Instead he had to call on Bob McClure, normally a starting pitcher, who walked Gene Tenace to load the bases and gave up a two-run single to Keith Hernandez. George Hendrick then drove across the go-ahead run.

By contrast, in the eighth inning Whitey Herzog of the Cardinals dispatched his ace reliever, Sutter, to replace Joaquin Andujar, who had given up three runs in the fifth and six innings; Sutter's split-finger fastball shut down the powerful Brewer batting attack to hold the lead and win the World Series for St. Louis.

The game's authorities seem to agree that those relief pitchers who enjoy greatest success are fitted to the demands of their profession temperamentally as well as physically. It is not necessary that the short reliever possess the arsenal of pitches that the starter must have. To win in the major leagues a starting pitcher must be master of at least two pitches, along with either the ability to change speeds frequently and effectively or else a third pitch such as the screwball, the slider, or the knuckleball. (The exceptions, of course, are the

Fellers, Groves, Ryans, and others who are gifted with such tremendous speed that for a time they need only an occasional curveball to keep the batters honest.)

The short reliever requires no such varied repertoire. He can be quite effective throwing only one particular pitch, especially if he can change speeds on it. Indeed, if he will be working for no more than one inning and he has an overpowering fastball, such as Goose Gossage possessed in his prime as a reliever for the Pirates and Yankees, he can come into the game and throw nothing but smoke, more smoke, and yet more smoke. This is particularly true when he enters in relief of a control pitcher who has been relying on curves and deception; the contrast will make it extremely difficult for even the best hitters to adjust the timing of their swing to accommodate the abrupt increase in pitching speed.

What the short reliever must have, of course, is the ability to throw strikes — to force the batter to swing at his pitches or else be called out. A relief pitcher without his control is a liability; not only will he be very likely put the potential tying or winning run on base, but in order to keep from walking a batter with the count full he may ease up slightly on a pitch and throw it down the middle of the plate, which is really all that a good hitter requires out of life.

The blinding speed of a Gossage, a Steve Bedrosian, a Ryne Duren, or a Lee Smith is all the more effective for being just a trifle erratic — not truly wild, but sufficiently unpredictable to install in the batter a more than customary apprehension of being hit by a pitch. Not only will the batter tend to back off a little, but to compensate for his nervousness he may chase pitches that are outside the strike zone. Duren's capacity for intimidating batters was enhanced by the thick-lensed spectacles he always wore; the man at the plate could never feel sure that the big right-hander saw him standing there.

Just as obviously, however, the relief specialist who pours in fastball after fastball, or slider after slider, with everything he has got, must get his man quickly, because it will not be long before the shock of having to confront such intimidating speed will wear off, and the batter will begin to time his swing to the speed of the pitch. When that happens, the ball will last be seen headed for the outfield fences.

Short relief, therefore, tends to become an all-or-nothing affair, and the pitchers who can handle it best are usually not the introverts of this world, who are constantly examining their motives and meditating upon the nature of mortality, but the free-and-easy, outgoing types who are delighted to lounge about the bullpen for several hours, jesting with their peers and scrutinizing the adjacent female scenery, and then be summoned hastily to get loose and prepare for immediate action. They are like the harpooners in *Moby Dick*, who as Melville said should be at the peak of their efficiency when abruptly called to their duty, and so "must start to their feet out of idleness, and not from out of toil."

For whatever reason, short relief pitchers tend to

be free spirits, given to practical jokes and irreverent attitudes toward constituted authority. Sparky Lyle of the Yankees was especially talented in this respect. (Lyle's book, *The Bronx Zoo*, has the distinction of being perhaps the most vulgar book ever written about major league baseball.) On one occasion the Yankees were playing a series in Baltimore, and shortstop Fred Stanley had made a good deal on a cheap silver-sprayed coffin, with the idea of converting it into a bar for his van. (And why would anyone wish to have a coffin for a bar? Talk about relief pitchers. . . .) Having no place else to keep it until he could ship it home, Stanley brought it into the visiting team's clubhouse, where it rested on a hand truck in the middle of the room.

Lyle secured a surgical mask with a hood that fit tightly over his head, bought some lampblack and rubbed it all around his eyes, climbed into the coffin during batting practice, and pulled the lid shut over him. When the team returned to the clubhouse, manager Bill Virdon began going over the Oriole batting lineup. Suddenly the coffin lid swung open and a spectral figure intoned, "But how doooo yoooooooo pitch to Brooks Ro-been-son?"

Most good relief pitchers seem to lose their form after several years. They are not usually young players, but veterans of some seasons of service. The ability to enter a baseball game in the late innings game after game and shut down the opposition would appear to result from the convergence of various skills. At a certain point in the pitcher's career everything begins to work together for him, and for three or four seasons the reliever is all but unbeatable. Then something happens, the fabric unravels, the competitive edge is lost, and the reliever begins giving up hits and runs on pitches that formerly fooled the batters. There are exceptions, such as Rollie Fingers and Lyle, but the records of baseball are crowded with the names of relievers who flourished spectacularly for several years, then abruptly lost their effectiveness.

This seems particularly true for the reliever who does his job by deception rather than by overpowering speed. In part it may be due to the simple fact that after a time he has made enough appearances for opposing batters to grow accustomed to his pitching. But it appears also to involve psychological factors, a state of mind that when it develops causes the pitcher to lose some of his aggressiveness. Whatever else may be true of a relief pitcher, he has got to feel cockily confident, even when he enters the game with no outs and runners on the bases, that no matter what difficulties the previous pitcher may have run into, he will be able to take care of everything. Once he begins to doubt that, he loses his edge.

There is no one way to get ready to hit a baseball, but when it comes to actually hitting it, only one way will do it properly. Meet the ball squarely, with the hips turning in with the swing to bring the body around and get the full force of its pivoting strength behind the blow. If the hip turns in a split second too early, then the arm muscles pull the bat down rather than forward, the arc of the swing is distorted, and the bat does not attain full velocity until it is past the point of contact with the ball. A split second too late, and the strength of the turning body is not applied to the swing, so that the extended forearm muscles alone must provide all the power. To hit a baseball well, the hips must act as a fulcrum for the pivoting muscles, and they cannot do this unless the shoulders are level, the batter's head is steady, and the front foot of the batter is firmly extended.

Whether the batter uppercuts the ball, as Ted Williams and Babe Ruth sought do do, or swings through it in accordance with Charlie Lau's theory, when the bat makes contact with the ball it must be with the weight of the turning body used to full advantage. How the batter gets his arms, legs, and torso in a position to do this, however, is a matter of individual preference, and there is certainly no agreement on methodology. The three leading batters of the 1940s and 1950s each had a different approach. Joe DiMaggio kept both legs well apart and anchored, and rotated his torso only. Ted Williams kept his feet fairly close together, then stepped into the pitch, in classic major league batting style. Stan Musial batted from a pronounced crouch, uncoiling his body as he strode forward. At the moment of contact of bat and ball, however, all three were doing the same thing: keeping their shoulders level, pivoting their hips just behind the swing, and planting their forward foot firmly so that their bodies could rotate upon it.

Willie Mays used a spread stance that resembled Joe DiMaggio's, but somewhat more closed. Preparing for the pitch he moved around considerably, and his body seemed to uncoil as he began his swing. Pete Rose hit from an exaggerated crouch and when he attacked the ball strode decisively into the pitch. Dave Parker, now of the Oakland Athletics, also uses a closed stance, and strides into the pitch; his stance is classically graceful. Jim Rice of the Boston Red Sox, an exceptionally strong man physically, keeps his head down and shifts his weight noticeably from rear to front leg as he steps forward. Carl Yastrzemski's stance was unusual in that he held the bat high and kept it pointed straight up; Yaz hit from a crouch, and he had to make a wide swing to connect with the ball. Despite this he was a contact hitter, using all fields.

One of the unusual batting stances in baseball history was that of Mel Ott, who despite his small build — 5'9", 170 pounds — was six times the National League leader in home runs. Ott had a way of lifting his forward leg as he prepared to swing, so that to a casual observer he might have seemed to be hitting off one foot. In actuality, however, he always lowered his front foot and planted it a split second before he began to bring his bat around.

The greatest power hitter of all time, Babe Ruth, kept his bat low and his feet close together. He swung up at the ball, and used his powerful wrists to jerk it high and far. His stride was of moderate length only, and when he swung he pivoted almost completely around. As might be expected, Ruth struck out often; Yankee fans enjoyed watching him miss the ball almost as much as hitting it.

Some batters prefer to stand close to the plate, crowding it; some like to stand well away. Some make a point of moving well forward in the batter's box, while others anchor themselves as far back in the box as possible. Indeed, not a few batters vary their position, forward or back, close or away, in accordance with the way that the pitcher is working. As the old farmer said when a youth confessed that he wanted to take a girl to the fair but did not know how to ask for a date, "son, there ain't no wrong way."

What a batting coach does is to watch a player's stance and swing carefully, to make sure that the bat is coming through properly. But it is considerably more complicated than just doing that. The batter must not only swing through properly at the ball, he must do it no matter where the pitch might be in the strike zone. A stance and positioning that on a waist-high pitch down the middle of the plate might produce a perfect swing may also make it extremely difficult for the batter to cope with one that comes in low and inside. And that will not do, because while a batter may hit a certain kind of pitch best, if he wants to survive against major league pitching there had better not be other kinds of pitches that he cannot handle at all. The word will quickly get around, and he will soon be an ex-major leaguer.

Most good batters are known to prefer certain kinds of pitches; so-and-so is a high ball hitter, you may hear a play-by-play broadcaster announce, while such-and-such likes to hit pitches that are thrown well down in the strike zone. This does not mean that either of them can keep his bat on his shoulder until he gets the kind of pitch he wants. If the opposing pitcher is reasonably skilled at his trade the one pitch that the batter will see thrown into his strike zone least often is the one that he prefers. What the batter must be able to do, therefore, is to swing through effectively at the kind of pitch he doesn't particularly like to get. And it is the hitting instructor's responsibility to work with them until he can do that, and to suggest changes in stance and positioning that will permit him to do it.

Naturally enough, this is more likely to happen with a young player not yet accustomed to handling major league pitching, than with a veteran. The difference between the pitching in the major leagues and even the high minors is the difference between pinpoint accuracy and approximation. To survive for very long, the major league pitcher must be able to deliver the baseball not only up or down in the strike zone, but close or away — and this with at least two good pitches, usually the fastball and the curve, and preferably a third as well. The batter must be prepared to hit sinkers, sliders, knucklers, screwballs — whatever the pitcher is offering. The batting stance that had served a young hitter so well in high school, college, and even in the higher minors, where he could simply lay off certain kinds of pitches not to his liking, may prove too vulnerable against major league pitching, and a good coach may suggest the use of a radically different stance.

Even the seasoned veteran, however, will frequently ask for help from a batting coach skilled in picking up flaws and mistakes. Anyone who has ever played golf with any regularity knows how fatally easy it is to drift unsuspectingly into bad habits. Drives that have been sailing satisfyingly 250 yards down the fairway abruptly acquire a slice, or stay close to the turn and begin rolling along the grass barely 175 yards out. The golfer has begun doing something he shouldn't be doing, whether in the way he grips the club, begins his backswing or comes down at the golf ball, spreads his feet, turns his body, or follows through. Until he, or a teaching pro, can diagnose what that something is and take steps to correct it, he will be off his game. (It has been remarked that golf is a game in which a man will hit one good drive and then dub the next seventeen, and thereupon declare that he is off his game.) Now if this can happen with a golfer, who after all is swinging at a stationary target when he gets ready to swing and with all the time he wishes to get properly positioned, then how much more vulnerable is a major league baseball player who must manage to get a round wooden bat solidly applied to a ball which is traveling toward him at 70, 80, 90 miles an hour or more, in a different location each time, and sometimes breaking, sometimes rising, sometimes sinking as it approaches!

Under such circumstances, the services of an experienced coach, adept at spotting irregularities, can be invaluable, and few are the major leaguers, no matter how good they are at hitting a baseball, who do not avail themselves of those consulting services. Dale Murphy, of the Atlanta Braves, is one of the most feared hitters in the majors, and regularly finishes at the top of the league or close to it in home runs and runs batted in. He has been playing major league baseball for twelve years. Yet he recently declared that not a day goes by during the season that he doesn't have to be corrected in batting practice.

V

BOYS WILL BE BOYS

Tommy Lasorda telling jokes in Spanish, Dodger Stadium, 1985

Shawon Dunston and Montreal Expos, Wrigley Field, 1986

*Conversation is the blood of baseball. It flows
through the game, an invigorating system of
anecdotes. Ballplayers are tale tellers who have
polished their malarkey and winnowed their wisdom
for years.*

                    Thomas Boswell

Robin Yount and Bob Uecker, County Stadium, 1986

Joe Garagiola and Red Sox, Anaheim Stadium, 1986

Before every game, both teams mingle around the batting cage, creating a bizarre atmosphere where one-liners, insults, nicknames, rumors about who's going to be traded or fired, practically fill the air. In truth, baseball may have spawned more lore in the dugout and by the cage than it has on the field.

Thomas Boswell

Dave Van Gorder and Jim Kaat, Dodger Stadium, 1985

Les Moss and Yogi Berra, San Diego-Jack Murphy Stadium, 1986

A narrative voice with conviction is often hard to find. But not in baseball. The minors teach two lost American arts: how to chew tobacco and how to tell a story.

Thomas Boswell

Eddie Milner, Mario Soto and Pedro Guerrero, Dodger Stadium, 1985

Hubie Brooks and Keith Hernandez, Shea Stadium, 1986

You try to make work habits sound. But you can't go out there like it's a serious business. You've got to be jovial to make it enjoyable for everyone else. I joke around, I have fun, I talk at the batting cage. Most of it's a rag session — everyone teases everyone. But as soon as it's a half hour before the game everyone shuts up and puts their mind on their work. It's kind of unique, really.

Ron Kittle

Cliff Johnson and Cecil Fielder, Fenway Park, 1986

All the fooling around loosens up the atmosphere before the game. We play 162 games a year and the pressures and tensions are there. You've got to vent your feelings one way or another, and this time before the game is the best way to do it.

Roger McDowell

As Reggie Jackson talks to the press, Jay Johnstone ties his shoelaces together, Yankee Stadium, World Series, 1981

Steve Bedrosian and Braves, Dodger Stadium, 1985

Milwaukee Brewers, Tiger Stadium, 1986

George Brett and reporter, Royals Stadium, 1985

Fernando Valenzuela, Dodger Stadium, 1985

Mets GM Frank Cashen and Gary Carter, Shea Stadium, 1986

Joe Torre, Gene Mauch and Moose Stubing, Royals Stadium, 1985

There's an incredible camaraderie. Except for maybe the extreme adrenalin that flows when you succeed on the field, the camaraderie and the banter that goes on between major league players is probably what the guys miss the most when they're out of the game.

Rusty Staub

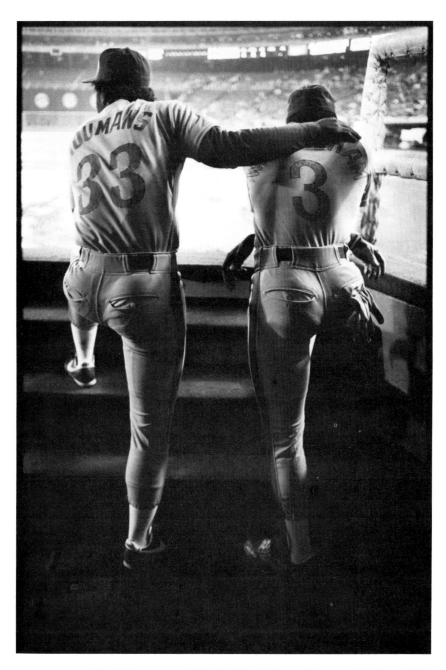

Floyd Youmans and Herb Winningham, Veterans Stadium, 1986

VI

PORTRAITS IN SOLITUDE

Mickey Rivers, Yankee Stadium, 1980

Once in a while I'll sit in the dugout and look out on the field and wonder what good is all this, thinking about me, me, me, my batting average, my fielding average. Oh, sure, you care about the team. You have to. But in the end you're worried about you.

Al Kaline

Paul Molitor, Tiger Stadium, 1986

Carl Yastrzemski, Yankee Stadium, 1980

Reggie Jackson, Yankee Stadium, 1980

Of all team sports, baseball, with its graceful intermittences of action, its immense and tranquil field sparsely settled with poised men in white, its dispassionate mathematics, seems to be best suited to accommodate, and be ornamented by, a loner. It is an essentially lonely game.

John Updike

Mike Schmidt, Veterans Stadium, 1986

Jim Rice, Fenway Park, 1986

Ron Cey, Wrigley Field, 1986

Sid Bream, Shea Stadium, 1985

Don Zimmer, Yankee Stadium, 1980

What do managers really do?
Worry. Constantly. For a living.
*   Leonard Koppett*

Earl Weaver, Tiger Stadium, 1986

Gene Mauch, Royals Stadium, 1985

Sparky Anderson, Yankee Stadium, 1986

*It's amazing how fast you grow
old in this game. At first you're
the rookie right-hander; next
season you're that promising
right-hander; then suddenly
you're the old man.*

Don Sutton

Vince Coleman in his rookie year, Shea Stadium, 1985

Bret Saberhagen before his first World Series start, Royals Stadium, 1985

George Scott in the last days of his career, Yankee Stadium, 1979

I remember the last season I played. I went home after a ballgame one day, lay down on my bed, and the tears came to my eyes. How can you explain that? It's like crying for your mother after she's gone. You cry because you love her. I cried, I guess, because I loved baseball and I knew I had to leave it.

Willie Mays

Frank Robinson, Fenway Park, 1986

The real moments of the game are invisible to people watching "baseball" because we are addicted to the familiar scenes, the camera cliches. But for all the great players and the cumulative intensity of the pennant race, there are a thousand times more instants of hollow repose, of dreaming out from the game, and of the gods battering away at the stale repetitious images through the irresistible power of their archetypes.

Richard Grossinger, writer

Rusty Staub, Shea Stadium, 1984

VII

FROM ONE GENERATION TO THE NEXT

Frank Howard and Rob Deer, Tiger Stadium, 1986

*I work with the young Tigers because I enjoy it and
feel like I'm repaying a debt. A lot of help was given
me by older players when I was a young man just
breaking into the big leagues. Now, I'm trying to pass
some of that along to the youngsters today. If I can
help someone — whether it's with his playing skills
or his attitude — that's a good feeling.*

Al Kaline

Bryan Kelly and Billy Muffett, Tiger Stadium, 1986

Jose Canseco and Bob Watson, Memorial Stadium, 1986

Johnny Grubb and fans, Tiger Stadium, 1986

You're part of a chain that goes back for generations passing the art along.

Sandy Koufax

Tommy Helms, Ryan Helms and Ron Robinson eating sunflower seeds, Dodger Stadium, 1985

Ron and Hayley Kittle, Comiskey Park, 1986

Mickey Mantle, Old Timers Day, Yankee Stadium, 1986

Baseball is a game dominated by vital ghosts; it's a fraternity, like no other we have of the active and the no longer so, the living and the dead.

Richard Gilman

Baseball is continuous, like nothing else among American things, an endless game of repeated summers, joining the long generations of all the fathers and all the sons.

Donald Hall

Father and son, Yankee Stadium, 1986

Getting old-timers, especially former players now in their late middle and elderly years, to admit that players of a later day are equal to or better than those of their own time is difficult. Major league baseball has a Golden Age, which always happens to be the years when the former player or fan remembering it was young. When I was in my teens the Golden Age that the old-timers looked back to was the Dead Ball Era of the 1900s and 1910s. A couple of decades later and the Golden Age was that of the 1920s. Now the Golden Age is the 1930s and 1940s.

What distinguishes baseball from other sports such as football or basketball, however, is that comparisons between different eras can be based on something more than subjective opinion. The continuity involved in major league baseball is such that it is quite possible to compare today's players with those of almost a century ago and more. The game hasn't changed nearly so much as has football or basketball, and moreover the statistics aren't merely relative but, within certain limits, absolute.

A professional football quarterback of a half-century ago played both defense as well as offense, and his season consisted of many fewer games than his counterparts of today play. Even more importantly, the number of passes he completed, or the number of yards he gained from scrimmage, depended importantly on how strong a line was protecting him, or opening holes in the defensive line. But in baseball the hitters on a good team face pitchers under approximately the same conditions as the hitters on a cellar-dwelling club, while the balance between good pitching and good hitting is weighted so heavily in favor of the pitcher that earned-run averages and even won-and-lost records can provide a reasonable gauge of a pitcher's effectiveness regardless of how mediocre the ball club behind him.

The game has remained the same over the decades in most important respects. If, for example, a luminary of today such as Mike Schmidt or Wade Boggs were somehow to find himself transplanted in time to the year 1910, and were to join a major league game, he could do so with almost no adjustment at all. His uniform might seem a trifle tight-fitting, his cap would have a larger crown and brim, and the number on the back would have no counterpart in those he saw around him on the field, but it would be recognizably a baseball uniform and not anything else. The glove he wore would be huge in comparison to the tiny leather affairs that did little more than protect the fingers. He would find it odd that the catcher probably did not wear shin guards.

Before the game was ready to begin, a powerfully-voiced announcer would go over to the grandstands and, shouting through a megaphone, announce the starting lineups — for there would be no public address system. The scoreboard in center field would have no electronic features.

The capacity of the grandstand and bleachers would be smaller, and if the game were an important one and there were no more seats available, the crowd would be allowed to spill over onto the playing field itself, standing behind ropes beyond the left- and right-field foul line and sometimes even along the center-field fence. Supposedly the ropes would be lowered and the crowd would make way for an outfielder pursuing a baseball, but if he were on the visiting team he could expect considerable difficulty in doing so.

The fans in the stands would be wearing hats or cloth caps, regardless of the time of year, and there would be very few female fans present, for a baseball stadium was not a respectable place for a lady to be seen in. No matter how hot it might be that day, the umpires would be fully attired in coat and tie. At most there would be two umpires working the game, one for balls and strikes, the other on the bases. Sometimes — though not often by then — there might even be only a single umpire, who, when runners were on base would come from behind the plate and take up his position behind the pitcher's mound. This could mean that if there were a close play at home plate to occupy the umpire's attention, impatient base runners were not above taking a short cut from first base to third by cutting to the inside of second base.

One thing that the modern player would certainly notice was that many of the players on both teams would be several inches shorter in height than himself. A player who was more than six feet tall would stand out prominently. There would be more than a few players on the team who were no more than five feet, four or five inches tall; if someone like Freddie Patek, the Kansas City Royals' second baseman of the 1970s, were to walk onto the field in 1910 his diminutive size would scarcely be cause for much comment.

When the batters came to the plate, they would grip their bats differently than the hitters of today. Not only would they choke up on the handle, but most of them would spread their hands so that there might be several inches separating them. As for the bats themselves, they would have thicker grips and would also weigh more than modern bats. The batting style would be somewhat different, too; even the heaviest hitters of the day would seem to chop and swipe at the ball instead of whipping the bat through the strike zone.

Once the game began the modern player would soon find that although the baseball being used became discolored and perhaps even developed nicks and scratches here and there, no move would be made to replace it. Indeed, if the ball disappeared over the fence, when a new one was put into play it would be passed around the infield and by the time it got to the pitcher would be dark from the application of tobacco juice.

The cover of the ball would also begin to soften up from the repeated impact of the bat, but this too would not seem to bother anybody. Not until the stitching on the seams began to fray would the umpire think it appropriate to replace it. Because the ball was softer it rebounded off the bat in a considerably less lively fashion than the modern player would be used to, and he would understand why it was that the outfielders were positioned closer to the infield than nowadays.

The playing area of the ballpark itself would be less symmetrical in shape than most fields the modern player would be used to seeing. Left and right field might be unevenly shorter, and center deeper, with the fence as far as 500 feet or more distant from home plate. So it would be considerably more difficult to hit home runs, especially with the softer baseball. Three-base hits, however, would be more common.

The modern player would notice that there was not as much attention paid to cutting off throws from the outfield or backing up plays at first, third, and home. When the defensive players came in to bat they left their gloves out on the field. Today's major leaguer would also observe that there were considerably fewer players on the bench and in the bullpen and that the coaching at first and third base was often handled by players rather than coaches.

Yet all these are superficial changes in the game, if compared to what has happened in other sports. Once the modern player became used to the greater emphasis on bunting, and the tactics involved in always playing for one run and never the big inning, he would have little difficulty in participating fully in the game as it was characteristically played eighty years and more ago. He would find that the best players of the 1900s and 1910s were every bit as good as those of today, although he would also feel, and with reason, that the second-line players tended to be less skilled and able than the journeymen players of his own time. The game they played, however, would be baseball pretty much as he knew it.

✕

The principal criticism lodged against major league baseball today is that the players are paid such huge salaries that they have become spoiled, and have lost some of their competitive zeal. And it is quite obvious that some of the salaries paid are excessive. That certain highly-paid stars have shown themselves to be petulant, self-centered, and childish is beyond question, and the fact that the long-standing reserve clause which placed a player in virtual bondage to his ball club has now been ruled illegal has clearly restricted the ability of the club to force the player to toe the line.

Yet that the game is being played with any less enthusiasm and zeal today than it was in the past, or that the players of today care less about winning ball games than their predecessors, is dubious. Since the earliest days of the game there have always been players who were more competitive, more dedicated to their profession than others, and likewise there have always been those who liked to dog it. That the quality of play in major league baseball today is not as high as in past years is on the face of it unlikely. And as for the oft-voiced complaint about players being unwilling any more to submit themselves to managerial direction and discipline, precisely the same charge was being voiced at all times in the past.

One man's golden age is another's iron time; when John McGraw bowed out as manager of the Giants in 1932, it was supposedly because the pampered athletes of then-modern baseball were no longer willing to subordinate their personal concerns to the greater good of the team. When Connie Mack broke up his championship Athletics of 1911-1914, it was because the stars had been spoiled by Federal League offers and were not giving their all any more.

In the 1960s the great Tyrus Raymond Cobb himself informed readers of the *Saturday Evening Post* that the players of the time were so intent on hitting home runs and making money that they no longer cared about anything else. And I have no doubt that Cap Anson, Abner Dalrymple, George Wright, Arlie Lathan, Hugh Duffy, and other luminaries of the nineteenth century said the same about the Cobbs, Youngs, Mathewsons, Johnsons, and Speakers.

Just for the sake of argument, let us grant that until after World War II baseball was the only major professional team sport, and so drew all the best athletes. Let us grant, too, that the number of players needed to staff 16 major league ball clubs is fewer then the number required to fill out the rosters of 26 clubs. Let us also grant that baseball played at night is harder on the eyes than baseball played in daylight, that to fly from Los Angeles to Chicago after a night game, arriving at O'Hare Airport at three A.M., climbing aboard a bus and checking in at a hotel downtown in the Loop, and then having to get going in time for an afternoon game at Wrigley Field the following day is hard on a ballplayer's constitution.

Let us, moreover, grant that without television sets in hotel rooms, players on road trips sometimes might have found little else to do in the evening except to sit around the hotel lobby and discuss the finer points of playing baseball. Finally, we will grant that high-salaried players can afford to purchase drugs, and that some have done so.

Consider, however, that the nation's population in 1920 was only half of what it is today, and also that today's major league teams draw heavily on players from Latin America as well. Which is harder on the constitution, a night game played with the temperature in the 70s and 80s, or an afternoon game with the sun bearing down on the playing field and the temperature in the high 90s? How restful was an all-night-and-half-the-day trip in a curtained-off berth in a non-air-conditioned pullman coach pulled by a steam locomotive that left behind it a cloud of smoke and cinders?

Remember, too, that all-night poker games, pool halls, saloons, burlesque theaters, movies, and red light districts were not exactly unknown to civilized man, and also that Crab Orchard, Four Roses, and rurally-distilled White Lightning could and did wreck many a promising baseball career back in the Good Old Days. Drugs may be slicker, but liquor is cheaper.

The most telling argument, however, against the notion that there has been a decline in the quality of baseball in the major leagues in the last thirty years is as follows:

Imagine, if you can, what the game would have been if the following players had been removed from the lineup: Henry Aaron, Felipe Alou, Ernie Banks, Don Baylor, Lou Brock, Roy Campanella, Rod Carew, Orlando Cepeda, Chris Chambliss, Roberto Clemente, Dave Concepcion, Andre Dawson, Larry Doby, George Foster, Bob Gibson, Dwight Gooden, Pedro Guerrero, George Hendrick, Bill Madlock, Reggie Jackson, Juan Marichal, Willie Mays, Willie McCovey, Willie McGee, Hal McRae, Joe Morgan, Manny Mota, Eddie Murray, Don Newcombe, Tony Oliva, Dave Parker, Tony Perez, Jim Rice, Frank Robinson, Jackie Robinson, Ozzie Smith, Willie Stargell, Maury Wills, Dave Winfield.

Until 1937, not one of those players, or any of the hundreds of other black Americans who have since appeared in major league baseball games, would have been allowed to do so.

So much, then, for the "Golden Age."

Before the game begins spectators are likely to see very little of the manager. During pre-game practice the manager usually stays in the dugout, talking with newspaper reporters, and in company with his coaches he draws up his lineup in terms of who the opposing team will be pitching that day. Most of the stronger hitters can handle left-handed or right-handed pitching with reasonable success; no manager worth his salt would for a moment consider benching a right-handed batter such as Andre Dawson or a left-handed batter like George Brett just because the opposing team's pitcher was right-handed or left-handed.

Other batters are not so versatile, and need to be platooned for maximum efficiency. A left-handed pitcher's curveball will come in toward a left-handed batter and then break away from him. So during the split second when the batter must decide whether to swing or not to swing at a pitch, his reflexes may tempt him to bail out in order to avoid being hit by the ball, only to have it curve across the plate for a called strike. Or he may delay his decision to swing just long enough to prevent him from meeting the ball solidly. The same pitch, thrown to a right-handed batter, will start outside and then break in toward him. The batter will thus have a fraction of a second longer to decide

what to do. If his reflexes do impel him to fall away from the plate it will be because the pitch is probably a ball inside.

In conference with his coaches the manager works out his strategy, decides who he will pinch-hit if a left-handed pitcher comes into the game in relief of a right-handed starting pitcher and so on, canvasses the availability of his own pitching staff and decides who will be sent to the bullpen, who will relieve early if needed, who will be the middle reliever, and so on.

To make such decisions, a manager may depend heavily upon pitching charts and statistical information. The Baltimore Orioles' Earl Weaver, for example, placed considerable reliance upon the statistics sheet furnished him before each game telling him how each of his players had fared against the scheduled opposing pitcher. Not only did Weaver use different batters against different pitchers, but he frequently altered the order in which his best hitters batted, in accordance with what the charts showed. During the 1970 season the Orioles once played a stretch of forty games during which there was a different starting lineup every day.

The choice of a lineup can involve a considerable battle of wits between opposing managers. No simple formula of pitting right-handed batters against left-handed pitching and vice versa will suffice. Each manager must think down the line, attempting to figure out what the opposing manager is likely to do, what and who will be available to counter such action, and so on.

In the 1924 World Series between the New York Giants and the Washington Senators, Bill Terry, a left-handed batter, was feasting upon Washington pitching, having already collected six doubles, a triple, and a home run in twelve official times at bat. So in the seventh game Manager Bucky Harris of the Senators started a right-handed pitcher, Curly Ogden, and then after Ogden had pitched to two batters replaced him with a left-hander, George Mogridge.

In the sixth inning the Senators had a 1-0 lead, and thus far Terry had grounded out and then taken a called third strike. So in the top of the sixth inning, after a leadoff walk, John McGraw, the Giants' manager, sent up the right-handed-batting Irish Meusel to pinch-hit for Terry. Whereupon Harris, having rid the Giants' lineup of Terry for the remainder of the afternoon, removed Mogridge from the mound and brought in right-hander Fred Marberry to pitch.

The strategy appeared to backfire when Meusel hit a sacrifice fly that scored a run and tied up the game. But as the contest wore on, Terry's hot bat was sorely missed by the Giants, especially after the game went into extra innings tied at 3-3. The Giants had runners on base in each of the 10th, 11th, and 12th innings, but were unable to score, and Washington won the game and the Series by scoring a run in the bottom of the 12th.

Had Harris not opened the game with a right-hander, McGraw would undoubtedly have started Meusel in the outfield, played George Kelly at first base, and saved Terry for a key pinch-hitting opportunity. Harris figured rightly that once Terry was in the game McGraw would leave him there even against a left-hander, but that if the game proved to be close, when the chips were down, the Giants skipper would play the percentages and opt for a right-handed batter even in replacement of the heavy-hitting but left-handed-batting Terry.

As might be guessed, the use of statistical data by managers in selecting their lineups has increased over the years. The kind of detailed information on opposing players' performances now available to an Earl Weaver and all other present-day skippers mostly did not exist in the earlier, pre-computerized years. Managers had to rely upon their own memories and advice from players and coaches. Joe McCarthy, who directed the mighty New York Yankee teams of the 1930s and early 1940s, was renowned among his players for his memory; he could recall the strengths and weaknesses of opposing batters in incredible detail.

Tommy Henrich told Donald Honig, author of *Baseball Between the Lines,* of one occasion in 1937 when the Yankees were playing Washington, and the Senators inserted Jimmy Wasdell, just up from the Southern Association, in their lineup. Red Ruffing, who was to pitch for New York that day, asked whether anyone knew anything about Wasdell. Although Henrich had played against him in the minors, he volunteered nothing, because he had "seen too many outfielders give well-meaning advice that exploded in somebody's face."

At that juncture McCarthy spoke up. "I know who he is," he said. "He's that kid that pinch-hit against us in Chattanooga when we came through there in the spring. He can't hit a change-up."

Henrich was astounded, both at the time and in retrospect. "I still don't believe a man can have that kind of memory," he told Donald Honig, deciding that McCarthy must have received a scouting report when Wasdell was elevated to the Washington roster. If so, the Yankee skipper was smart enough to let his players believe he could recall the batting flaws of someone who had pinch-hit against the Yankees once in an exhibition game. Wasdell's weakness *was* indeed change-ups. He went 0 for 4 that day, and though he played in the major leagues for parts of eleven seasons never became a hitting star.

McCarthy once visited his long-time Yankee third baseman, Red Rolfe, after Rolfe had become manager of Detroit, and observed numerous clipboards hanging about Rolfe's office, on which Rolfe kept elaborate records of what had happened in various games. That, McCarthy told Tommy Henrich, was what was wrong with Rolfe as a manager: he had a very poor memory.

It is generally agreed that what a manager does for a living, more than anything else, is *worry*. There are so many things about the game of baseball that he cannot control. Somebody once asked Frank Frisch why it was that baseball managers grew grey. "Bases on balls!" Frisch responded with fervor. "Bases on balls!" To have to watch, in a close game, while one's pitcher issues a base on balls to the leadoff man in a late inning, thus putting the winning run on base with nobody out, is hard on the nerves and the digestion alike.

There is no *reason* for the pitcher to hand out an advantage like that to the opposing team; even if the pitch had been thrown down the middle of the plate there would at least have been the chance that the batter would ground out or hit a fly ball to the outfield. A major league pitcher, being paid a salary in six figures, who cannot throw strikes when needed, is a grievous phenomenon for a manager to contemplate. The manager can plan all he wishes, prepare elaborate strategies, yet if his players do not execute, he is helpless.

The technique of managing a major league club varies from individual to individual, and sometimes from game to game. What works with some personnel will not work with others. One team may have an abundance of talent on its roster, yet as a team lack sufficient competitive zeal. Another may be so riddled with dissention, so divided at each other's throats, that it cannot devote its full energies to defeating its opponents. If the teams in question are to begin winning, a change in managerial tactics will obviously be required.

Billy Martin, several times in the past and now once again the manager of the New York Yankees, has shown himself a master at rallying the sagging spirits of a hitherto-indifferent ball club, getting the players to believe in themselves and in the possibility of playing winning baseball, and thus converting hitherto-mediocre ball clubs into pennant contenders. If, therefore, a club owner desires to build a fire under complacent or discouraged ballplayers, and Billy Martin is without employment at the time, firing the present manager and hiring Martin is worth considering. Various ball clubs have done so in the past — the Texas Rangers, Minnesota Twins, Detroit Tigers, Oakland A's, and — on what are now four separate occasions — the New York Yankees.

On each occasion the results have been both startling and gratifying to club owner and fans — for a brief period. Unfortunately Martin doesn't know where to stop stirring — or more properly, the same character traits that enable Martin to restore vigor and competitiveness to a lackadaisical ball club also act to make him push his players too hard. Healthy competitiveness begins turning into bitter rivalry, dislikes become hatreds, and individual nerves grow so taut and frayed that the team begins to beat itself rather than its opponents. Thus Martin has again and again made losing teams into winners, only to get himself fired after it happens. No prudent betting man would give odds on Billy Martin's present tenure as skipper of the Yankees lasting notably longer than his previous managerial stands at Yankee Stadium. If, as has been reported, Martin's recent marriage has been so very good for him that the combative returning skipper of the Yankees has been able to adopt a more philosophical attitude toward managing ballplayers and working for George Steinbrenner, a pleasant surprise may be in store for all concerned. But don't count on it.

Martin was the co-star in one of the more bizarre affirmations ever staged of the old adage that major league managers are hired to be fired. The clash of temperaments between George Steinbrenner and whoever happens to be the Yankee manager at the time has made the tenure of office at Yankee Stadium precarious as never before in baseball history. Steinbrenner has changed managers in much the same way motorists change oil: every six months or three thousand miles, whichever comes first.

In contrast to Dr. Martin's strenuous, combative temperament was the calm, reassuring managerial style of the man who became first his successor and then his predecessor with the Yankees of the Steinbrenner era, Bob Lemon. As a player, Lemon had been far more successful than Martin, who was at best a garden-variety infielder for the Yankees under Casey Stengel in the 1950s. Lemon had begun his career as an infielder, then converted into a sinker-throwing right-handed pitcher who won 207 ball games for the Cleveland Indians between 1946 and 1958, seven times winning 20 games or more in a season.

In mid-July of 1978 Lemon took over a Yankee club that was 14 games out of first place. Shaken by dissention between Martin and Reggie Jackson, and demoralized by the public feuding between Steinbrenner and Martin, the World Champion Bronx Bombers were going nowhere. Lemon calmed things down, got his greatly talented club playing together as a team, and overhauled the Boston Red Sox to win a one-game playoff for the divisional championship. The Yankees then demolished the Kansas City Royals to take the American League pennant and in the World Series overcame a two-game deficit to defeat the

Los Angeles Dodgers and win the championship.

In the season following, however, Lemon began to lose control of his club — in part because the death of his only son in an accident had caused him to begin drinking heavily — and the highly volatile Steinbrenner thereupon replaced him with Martin. Two years later, in 1981, Lemon took over the Yankees shortly before the end of the second half of a strike-divided season, and had the pleasure of demolishing the Oakland A's, now managed by Martin, in the divisional playoffs, before losing to the Los Angeles Dodgers in the World Series. Before even the end of the first month of the 1982 season Lemon was gone again, replaced this time by the man he had replaced the year before, Gene Michael. (Michael had taken over in 1981 after the late Dick Howser, despite having won a pennant the year before, had been fired and Clyde King, Steinbrenner's troubleshooter, had finished out the season. King's numerous friends were relieved when he did not continue on as manager for the next season, given the ways of his employer.)

Although Steinbrenner's impatience has made managing the New York Yankees an especially unstable mode of employment, swift hiring and abrupt firing has always been an occupational hazard of managing in the major leagues. As has frequently been remarked, it is considerably easier to terminate the services of one manager than of two dozen players, so if at any given time a team isn't doing especially well, the obvious remedy is to fire the person in charge.

Casey Stengel, having himself been fired as manager of the Brooklyn Dodgers and then the Boston Braves, knew from personal experience just how unrealistic were the grounds on which most major league skippers lose their jobs. In 1949 he was made manager of the pre-Steinbrenner Yankees, and for the first time in his career had some really good ballplayers on his club. From that year until 1960, when he again lost his job supposedly for having grown too old (he was 70, but his team had won the pennant again that year), Stengel won ten out of a possible twelve American League pennants. On one occasion in 1950 Casey was a speaker at a dinner when the Pittsburgh Pirates' skipper, Bill Meyer, was present. Meyer had taken over the Pirates and brought them from a last-place finish in 1947 to fourth place in 1948, a feat which earned him a National League Manager of the Year award. In 1949, however, the Pirates had slipped to sixth place in the standings. "Billy," said Stengel, "what I can't understand is how I got smart so fast, and you got so dumb."

It is possible for a manager to get fired from his job even though his team wins not merely a pennant, as the Yankees did in 1960 under Stengel, but a world championship. In 1926 the St. Louis Cardinals, under player-manager Rogers Hornsby's leadership, stunned the baseball cosmos by taking the World Series from the mighty New York Yankees of Babe Ruth and Lou Gehrig, four games to three. It was the first St. Louis pennant ever, and Hornsby was the idol of the town. The World Series was scarcely over, however, before Hornsby, who in addition to being baseball's best right-handed hitter was a blunt, tactless soul, began quarreling with the Cardinals' owner, Sam Breadon. Hornsby had already earned Breadon's ire by ordering him out of the Cardinal clubhouse once while the players looked on. Now he accused Breadon of being tight-fisted and money-hungry. The quarrel developed in intensity over the winter, until at last Breadon had had enough, and traded his .400-hitting, World Series-winning manager to the Giants. As might be expected, the St. Louis sportswriters and fans were shocked when the news broke, and Frank Frisch, who came to the team as Hornsby's replacement at second base, was roundly booed for a time. The Cardinals, however, finished in second place in 1927 and won the pennant again in 1928, and Hornsby's departure was soon forgotten.

×

Perhaps the most astounding change of managers ever in major league history happened in 1948. What was shocking was not so much the firing of the incumbent skipper as the hiring of his replacement.

As outfielder on the New York Giants from the mid-1920s onward, Mel Ott was perhaps the most popular player ever to wear a Giant uniform, and when late in 1942 he was named manager, succeeding Bill Terry, there was great rejoicing among all Giant fans. But the Giants did not thrive. In 1946 they finished in last place for the second time in three years.

To make matters worse, their interborough rivals the Brooklyn Dodgers were flourishing as never before. For decades the Dodgers had been known mostly for their ineptitude. But after Larry MacPhail took charge of the franchise in 1938, things began to change. In 1939 he named Leo

Durocher as manager, and the brash, belligerent Durocher, making skillful use of the high-quality player personnel that MacPhail had been assembling, soon had the Dodgers in contention. In 1941 the Dodgers won the National League pennant, and except for one seventh-place finish during the war they were in the thick of competition for first place each season, with Branch Rickey replacing MacPhail at the top.

Abrasive, braggadose, loud-mouthed, Durocher seemed to personify everything that the modest, gentlemanly Mel Ott was not. In a famous exchange at the Polo Grounds during the 1946 season, Durocher was chided by reporters for his lack of generosity of spirit. "Why don't you be a nice guy for a change?" he was asked. Durocher leaped to his feet. "Nice guys!" he declared, pointing toward the New York Giant dugout. "Look over there. Do you know a nicer guy than Mel Ott? Or any of the other Giants? Why, they're the nicest guys in the world! And where are they? In last place!"

The comment, needless to say, did not sit well with the Giants and their fans, and it was only one of numerous ungentlemanly comments by Leo during his tenure in Ebbets Field. What made the Dodgers manager's outburst so difficult for the Giants and their partisans to take was the fact that Mel Ott and his nice guys *were* indeed in last place, and all too likely to remain there or close to it. The days of glory had departed from the Polo Grounds, and the Dodgers were not only in the habit of beating up on the Giants regularly, but of sprinkling salty rhetoric into the wounds. There was no justice in it.

In 1947 the Dodgers won the pennant, but

without Durocher, for his off-the-field actions and associations and his public pronouncements had earned him a one-year suspension by Baseball Commissioner Happy Chandler. The season following found Durocher back at the helm. But by early summer things were not going well at Ebbets Field. The Dodgers weren't winning, Durocher's mouth was earning him new enemies, and there was much dissension in the clubhouse. Meanwhile, across the river at Coogan's Bluff the Giants were foundering, and it had become obvious to owner Horace Stoneham that Mel Ott had to go.

Now Horace Stoneham, the Giants' owner, was no George Steinbrenner; he made managerial changes only with great reluctance, he was loyal to his manager and players, and he would never dream of criticizing his team in public. But clearly the Giants were going nowhere, and were likely to continue to do just that for years to come under Ott. So, knowing that despite his having won the pennant the year before, the Dodgers' interim manager Burt Shotton was currently without employment other than as a scout, Stoneham asked Branch Rickey for permission to talk to him. To Stoneham's surprise, Rickey proposed instead that he hire Durocher.

Thus on July 16, 1948, the news came out that the beloved Mel Ott had been discharged as manager of the New York Giants, and that — now get this — *his replacement was to be Leo Durocher!* The shock waves reverberated from coast to coast. It was as if George Washington had divorced Martha and married Peg Wolfington, or Mae West had been assigned to a film role previously played by Shirley Temple. It boggled the national consciousness, producing a *crise de confiance* in the hearts of long-faithful Giant fans. Men and women who had remained steadfast throughout the years of defeat, who had held to their allegiance despite the triumphant sneers of Dodger fans, now asked themselves whether it was indeed possible to continue. That Leo the Lip Durocher, this hoodlum, this renegade, this slob who for ten years had heaped insult upon all that was pure and holy, had trampled upon virtue, mocked the upright and godly, scoffed at nice guys — that this man, of all men, would now be manager of the New York Giants! As one thoughtful Dodger fan was quoted as observing when asked what he thought of what had happened, "Jeez! It's Poil Harbor for da Giants!"

The analogy was apt. Within two years Leo Durocher had cleaned house, gotten rid of the Giants' stable of ponderous sluggers, assembled a team that was swift and scrappy and opportunistic, and put the Giants into the pennant race. In 1951 Bobby Thomson hit the shot heard round the world into the lower deck of the left-field stands at the Polo Grounds, and the Giants were in the World Series. Three years later, with Willie Mays leading the way, the Giants swept a four-game Series from the favored Cleveland Indians and were champions of the world. So if July 16, 1948, was Pearl Harbor at the Polo Grounds, then October 2, 1954, was V-J Day.

Without good players, no major league manager can do very much for very long, and the only way that a manager of a second division team can keep his job for more than a couple of years is to own the ball club himself. The late Connie Mack is considered to be one of the game's all-time great managers. But when he broke up the splendid Philadelphia Athletics team which had won pennants in 1910, 1911, 1913 and 1914, American League fans in Philadelphia enjoyed the pleasure of seven straight last-place finishes before Mack's club again finished as high as seventh in the league standings. Again in 1932 Mack decided to begin selling off all the stars of the 1929-1931 club, and once more the Athletics dropped out of contention and remained out for the next two decades, finishing either last or next-to-last fourteen times. Mack could get away with it because nobody could do anything about it; the team was his private property, he ran it on a shoestring budget, and if the fans didn't show up at Connie Mack Stadium he could make ends meet by selling off promising ballplayers to other clubs. When the franchise was moved to Kansas City in 1955 it was the end of a long tradition of losing baseball, interrupted briefly by two great clubs but otherwise a dismal affair.

The truth is that while major league managers get the credit for winning pennants and world championships, and get fired when their teams don't keep winning, it is the general manager, the owner, or whoever does the hiring, firing, and trading that is responsible for first-rate baseball teams. Durocher was able to turn the Giants into a winning team because Horace Stoneham let him develop his own club. Casey Stengel became a managerial genius at the age of 58, after several decades of being a mediocrity, because George Weiss and the Yankee front office supplied him with good players. And when in 1965, after more than a half-century of winning baseball, the Yankees suddenly plummeted from first to last place and remained out of the running for a decade, it was because Weiss was gone and nobody else had come along to take his place and keep the good young players coming.

Despite the mania for statistics that is so much a part of the charm of major league baseball, to my knowledge nobody has ever developed a chart comparing the won-and-lost records of the game's chief executives. It would be interesting indeed to learn how many pennants were won and how many first-division finishes were earned by the various persons who directed the affairs of ball teams over the years. To be meaningful, however, the tenure being measured would have to cover at least a half-dozen years following the end of the individual general manager's employment, for a significant number of the players he will have recruited will not have made their impact on the game until then.

I feel certain that if such a comparison were made, the executive who would come out with highest marks would be the late Branch Rickey. The Mahatma, as he was called, not only invented the farm system, changed baseball scouting from a haphazard affair of unsystematic wandering about the country into a thoroughgoing search for talent, and ended the color line in 1947 by inserting Jackie Robinson into the Brooklyn lineup, but before that he had built the St. Louis Cardinal franchise from a losing proposition into an organization that from the mid-1920s until the late 1940s was almost always at or near the top of the National League standings. In the early 1940s Rickey moved on to Brooklyn, and building upon Larry MacPhail's winning but somewhat shaky foundation, gave the Dodgers a steady flow of talent that was still producing winning ball teams long after the franchise was moved to Los Angeles.

When in 1950, Rickey lost out to the machinations of Walter O'Malley, he transferred his operations to the Pittsburgh Pirates, a franchise that had not known success since the middle 1920s. After six years with the Pirates he retired, with his ball club still in last place. Within three years, however, it was battling for the National League pennant, and thereafter remained in contention for years, mainly on the strength of the young ball players that Branch Rickey and his staff of skilled scouts had signed to contracts, and who when he left were still engaged in learning their trade in the minor leagues.

When you take a seat in a major league ballpark you will probably not so much as catch sight of the general manager. He will be watching the game from a private, glassed-in booth somewhere, or for that matter may not be in attendance at all that day. But most of what you see before you on the field will be there because he willed it.

The starting pitchers are throwing hard now. The playing field is ready to go. The grounds crew has dragged the infield, watered it, raked and smoothed the areas around the bases, removed the soiled California-style bases from their sockets and replaced them with fresh bases, curried the terrain around home plate, and applied fresh lime to the foul lines and blocked out and limed the batters boxes. Now the umpires emerge from the dugouts and move toward home plate. There are a few mild boos from the crowd, which as game time nears has been steadily filing into the stands. The organist plays several bars of "Three Blind Mice."

The managers of the two teams go out to join the umpires. There are handshakes, an exchange of copies of the batting orders, and the ground rules for the ballpark are reviewed. The effort is to cover absolutely everything that might conceivably play a role in the outcome of the game if a batted or thrown ball were to come into contact with it. Overhead cables, guy wires, light poles, gates and alleys, railings, signs, tarpaulins, anything — each park has its own unique features, and at some point some time a baseball is going to end up in some place where its advent might otherwise cause a dispute if not agreed upon ahead of time. Yet no matter how thorough the review, or how elaborate the list of contingencies, there will be something overlooked or unexpected that can happen.

In baseball, there is a rule for everything, evolved over the course of 150 years and more. No umpire would dare carry onto the field with him a copy of the rule book; if challenged by an irate manager on his interpretation of a rule, the very last thing he wants to do is to engage in a session of *explication de texte* while the game is held up. He is supposed to have mastered the rules, and the rules are supposed to cover all contingencies.

Again, however, to do that is an impossibility. There will always be something.

And as we have seen, the rules change. Until 1931 a home run hit out of the playing field was fair or foul according to where it was when the umpire last saw it, rather than where it was located when it left the playing field, as nowadays. Until that same year a batted ball which bounced into the stands or over a fence or through a crack in the fence counted as a home run. Prior to 1921 all pitchers were allowed to employ saliva, slippery elm, licorice, or whatever to make a baseball perform tricks; now the spitball is illegal — which is not to say that it is not used. Before 1894 a batter could use a flat-surfaced bat to hit a ball. And so on. Each winter the rules committee meets to discuss further changes; most are very minor indeed.

The game, to repeat, has changed relatively little. The last really fundamental changes occurred in the 1880s and 1890s, when the pitcher's mound was moved to *sixty* feet, *six* inches from home plate, foul balls were charged to the batter as strikes, four balls became a base on balls, three strikes became a strikeout, and the batter was no longer allowed to call for a high or low pitch. Since then, for longer than what is now almost a full century, the game has retained its basic structure, so that, as suggested earlier, not only the player but the fan who was able, by some incredible bending of the light rays, to view a baseball game in the 1900s and 1910s would find little there that was unfamiliar.

There have been occasional proposals for basic changes. Perhaps the use of the designated hitter for the pitcher in the American League might fall into that category, though it hardly seems revolutionary. Some have suggested that the distance between bases be increased, which is to say, that first and third bases be moved further from home plate. The increased reach of the average infielder, and the development of large gloves with deep pockets, have made it extremely difficult to hit the ball through the infield on the ground. Another suggested innovation has been to place the pitcher's rubber further back. It seems safe to say that no such changes are likely to take place any time soon — not for as long as the game continues to attract fans in record numbers. For many years baseball used to be "the only game in town." Now it is only the best.

The umpires and managers have reviewed the ground rules. The teams are ready. Along the sidelines the starting pitchers are completing their warmups. "Ladies and gentlemen," intones the PA announcer, "will you please stand and honor America by joining in the singing of our national anthem!" There is a vast shuffling of feet and doffing of hats as crowd, players, coaches, umpires, officials, all who are in the ball park rise to their feet and stand facing the flagpole beyond center field, where the Stars and Stripes waves in the breeze or else hangs limply, depending on atmospheric conditions.

The custom of singing the "Star-Spangled Banner" before athletic events is not a ritual that goes far back into the history of the republic. Except for special occasions such as the opening game of the

World Series, it came into general use only during World War II, as a testimony of allegiance to a nation at war. In the 1950s it might have been discontinued but for the rise of the suspect-thy-neighbor stuff of the McCarthy Era, when American citizens felt obliged to demonstrate their soundness on the issues of the Cold War and the more super-patriotic types liked to demonstrate their superiority by singing several verses of the National Anthem rather than just the first. Fortunately, and especially given the vocal-chord-cracking nature of the notes in the next-to-last line, the baseball owners did not succumb to the last-named.

There are many who feel that to sing the "Star-Spangled Banner" on every occasion whatever cheapens it. Save it, they say, for times when it will be truly meaningful. I confess that it doesn't offend me at all to have it played and sung, although the practice of inviting popular figures from show business to sing it in syncopation or rock-and-roll-style I find annoying. A little "lah-a-ah-ah-nd of the free-ee-ee" goes a long way. When someone like Rocco Scotti, James Merrill, or Leontyne Price gives it the full operatic treatment, however, singing it straight and invigoratingly, it can still send the shivers down this senior citizen's spinal column.

Baseball is a game to play and an art to watch, and the more you know about it the more you enjoy it. Most people have played it at one time or another during their childhood, and understand enough of what is going on to recognize the highlights. The significance of a home run is clear, and that of a home run with the bases loaded obvious. A strikeout, a double play, a fine catch are for everyone to enjoy. Beyond that, how much knowledge is brought to bear will determine the richness of the viewer's involvement. The average spectator appreciates some things, but not as many as does someone who has played the game and studied its intricacies. Sportswriters who cover the game regularly understand more than most readers of newspaper sports stories, but the ballplayers themselves, the coaches, and the managers understand more than either.

Ring Lardner, who was a sports journalist before he became a humorist and a writer of fiction, tells of how, having reported on minor league baseball for the South Bend, Indiana, *Times*, he aspired to a job covering the major leagues in Chicago. In company with Hugh Fullerton, Sr., he attended the opening game of the 1907 World Series between the Cubs and the Detroit Tigers. There were runners on first and second, no outs, and Ty Cobb at bat:

Brownie [Mordecai Brown], whose control was perfect, threw the first one so high that Ty would have been insane to offer at it. I heard a couple of reporters suggest a possible purposeful pass. I knew better than that. A man with Brownie's brains is not deliberately filling the bases with Claude Rossman swinging two bats and the score nothing-all, or close to that figure. The purpose of the unbuntable ball was to see what the runners were apt to do, provided it was pitched within Cobb's reach. The runners had both been on the run and had to scramble back to escape death at the hands of [catcher] John Kling, sharpshooter. I expressed this theory to Hughey, whose reply thrilled me.

"You're ready for this league," he said. "But also, if they did start running, there was a good chance for Johnny to nail one of them."

The more you understand, to repeat, the more there is to enjoy. Here is a situation. With a slow runner, Jones, at first base, two outs, and the count 3-1 on a good hitter, the order comes from the bench for Smith, the batter, to take the next pitch for a strike. Smith keeps his bat on his shoulder, the pitcher grooves an extremely hittable fastball down the middle for a strike, and the crowd boos. "That bum," declares one observer to another. "He won't get many pitches like that to hit." Why would Smith pass up so very attractive a ball? Did he want a base on balls so badly that, rather than take a chance on swinging and possibly missing, he did not swing at all?

The next pitch comes in and Smith slaps it into left-center for a base hit. Jones, who had taken off for second with the pitch, keeps going and scores from first base.

What the people in the stands did not realize is that before Jones could race for second with the pitch without danger of being thrown out, there had to be a full count on the batter. And the only way Jones, being slow, could score all the way from first on a two-base hit would be if he were already

in motion toward second when the ball was hit. So that, and not timidity, stupidity, or the inability to recognize a hittable pitch, was why Smith took the 3-1 pitch for a second strike.

There was no possible way that a spectator could have known about the signal given to Smith. But the equation the spectator might have posed to himself is this: I know that Smith, the batter, is a competent professional, who earns a quite decent living hitting major league pitching. There must have been some reason why, with the count at 3-1, and knowing that the pitcher was going to have to come in with the ball in order to avoid putting a second runner on base, Smith did not so much as try to hit the pitch. What could it have been?

This is not to say, of course, that ballplayers do not sometimes think poorly if at all, and do not make mistakes. And it is not to say that the strategy being used always works. What if Smith had hit the 3-2 pitch directly at an infielder? With a 3-1 count the pressure was on the pitcher to come in with a good pitch; if he missed, the batter became a baserunner. But when Smith took the pitch for a strike the balance shifted; with two strikes on him he had to avoid striking out, while the pitcher could take a chance on throwing him a pitch that was harder to hit. So Smith's manager had to decide whether the opportunity to score the runner from first base was worth the risk of making Smith forego what was sure to be a good pitch to hit and take his chances on a less hittable ball.

If Smith had been given the green light on the 3-1 pitch and the slow-running Jones had made it only to third base, then what would be the prospects of the batter who followed Smith being able to hit the ball and score Jones from third? And suppose in that instance the opposition had decided to give an intentional base on balls to him, and work on the next batter; was *he* likely to be able to produce?

The man in the dugout has to decide. Today both he, and the man in the other team's dugout, have made their initial choices, decided upon a starting lineup, chosen their pitchers. Now the home team goes sprinting out onto the diamond, while the crowd cheers happily. The pitchers and catchers who will be held in reserve that day make their way along the sidelines out to the bullpen. The starting pitcher, having doffed his jacket, moves out to the mound, rearranges with his spikes a bit of the ground out where his foot will be striding, makes his warm-up throws to the catcher. The first baseman flips grounders to the infielders, who fire them back at him. The left fielder and center fielder make long throws to each other, while a bullpen catcher throws back and forth with the right fielder.

The practice baseballs are returned to the dugout. The coaches at first and third bases take their places. The leadoff batter, swinging several bats, stands by to hit, and the on-deck batter, kneeling on one knee, takes a practice swing or two. The PA announcer gives the position, uniform number, and name of the first hitter.

The pitcher makes his final warm-up throw; the catcher rifles the ball down to second base.

The catcher flashes his signal to the pitcher.

The batter has stepped in now, has scraped away a portion of the rear marking line of the box, has planted the heel of his back foot solidly, has taken his stance, flexed his arms, waved the bat about for a bit, and now is holding it at the ready.

The umpire behind home plate leans over the catcher's shoulder.

In the nine-inning format that is about to unfold, anything can happen: a pitcher's duel, a no-hitter, a slugfest, a lopsided score, or a close contest.

The hours of pitching and batting and fielding practice, and the weeks and months and years of individual and team experience, are now history: this day's baseball game is about to begin.

You are there with the others, in the stands, watching, waiting. How many hundreds, even thousands of baseball games have you seen in the past?

Yet this one will be different from all the others, for it is today's game.

At that moment a couple, a man and a woman, settle into the seats next to yours.

"They haven't started playing yet," one of them declares.

"Oh, goody!" says the other. "Then we haven't missed a thing!"

VIII

TAKE ME OUT TO
THE BALLGAME

Going up the ramp, Wrigley Field, 1986

*T**he first big league game I ever saw was at the Polo Grounds. My father took me. I remember it so well — the green grass and the green stands. It was like seeing Oz.*

John Curtis, pitcher

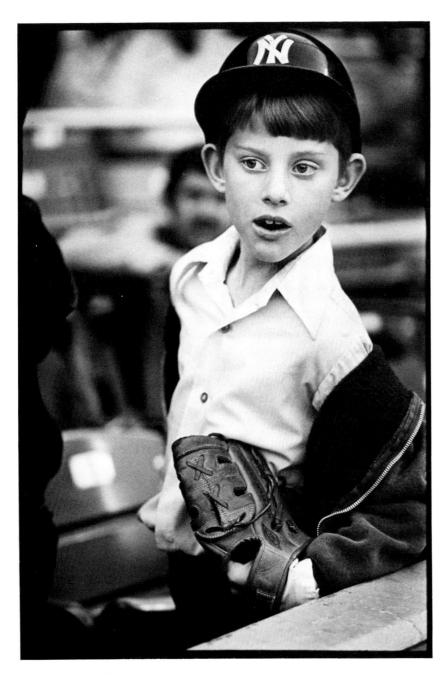

Yankee fan, Yankee Stadium, 1980

Watching batting practice, Fenway Park, 1986

Fenway fans, Fenway Park, 1986

*A*ll baseball fans can be divided into two groups:
Those who come to batting practice and the others.
Only those in the first category have much chance
of amounting to anything.

                            Thomas Boswell

Dodger fans, Dodger Stadium, 1985

Watching batting practice, Tiger Stadium, 1986

Cubs fans, Wrigley Field, 1986

Cardinals fan, Busch Stadium, World Series, 1985

Two fans and Wally Joyner, Memorial Stadium, 1986

I get more fan mail now than I ever did. I get letters now that almost make you cry. They tell me that looking up to me gave them inspiration to become what they are.

Mickey Mantle

Fan meets Lou Piniella, Yankee Stadium, 1980

Getting an autograph, Veterans Stadium, 1986

Waiting for an autograph, Fenway Park, 1986

Mickey Rivers and fans, Yankee Stadium, 1979

That one little piece of paper — although it may be thrown away an hour later — at that moment was special. The fan and the athlete came together in a personal way.

Steve Garvey

I think I have signed some scrap of paper for every man, woman and child in the United States.

Vida Blue

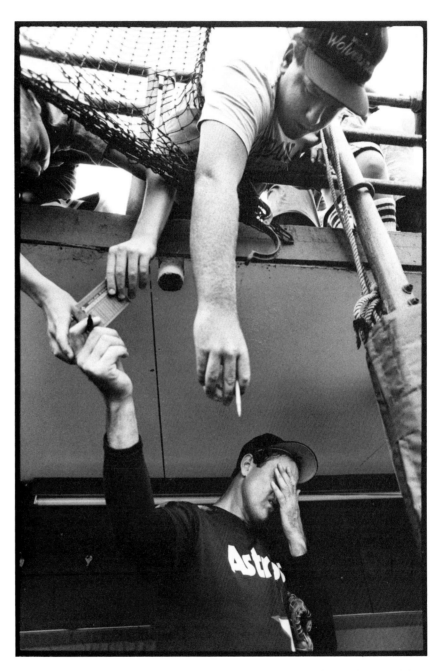

Autograph seekers and Nolan Ryan, San Diego-Jack Murphy Stadium, 1986

IX

THE DAILY SOAP OPERA

Baseball is the best sport for a writer to cover because it's daily. It's on-going. You have to fill the need, write the daily soap opera.

Peter Gammons, sportswriter

Don Zimmer and the press, Yankee Stadium, 1980

Ron Darling, Shea Stadium, 1985

Carmelo Martinez, Shea Stadium, 1986

No other sport has anything like the pre-game ritual of baseball. From a writer's point of view, it is invaluable. The writers are part of the team, not as rooters, one would hope, but as a presence. Players trust you with little details, little secrets, and sometimes even important observations, that eventually help make baseball a real thing to fans. In all other sports, a writer can show up at a game and miss nothing. In baseball, to miss the pre-game workout is not to be attuned to the club.

George Vecsey

Gary Carter, Shea Stadium, World Series, 1986

Once an athlete feels the peculiar thrill that goes with victory and public praise, he's bewitched. He can never get away from it.

Ty Cobb

Jerry Mumphrey, Yankee Stadium, World Series, 1981

Pete Rose being honored for breaking record, Dodger Stadium, 1985

Tommy Lasorda being sketched by Leroy Neiman, Yankee Stadium, 1981

Reggie Jackson, Yankee Stadium, 1980

Reggie Jackson, Yankee Stadium, American League Championship Series, 1981

He seems to carry a stage with him everywhere.
           Thomas Boswell on Reggie Jackson

Graig Nettles, Yankee Stadium, World Series, 1981

Graig Nettles, Yankee Stadium, 1980

Keith Hernandez, Shea Stadium, World Series, 1986

Batting cage, Shea Stadium, World Series, 1986

*I wish they'd shut the gates, and let us play ball with
no press and no fans.*

> *Dick Allen*

Roger Clemens, Shea Stadium, World Series, 1986

Joaquin Andujar, Shea Stadium, 1985

A ballplayer could go to college and be a sportswriter. But what writer could be a ballplayer?
                                                   Billy Martin

Frank White, Royals Stadium, World Series, 1985

THE STAGE LIGHTS DIM

Tiger Stadium, 1986

Batboy, Royals Stadium, 1985

*Especially at evening, when the sky itself darkens
like the stage lights dimming, there is a co-existence
of total relaxation and keen anticipation that is
totally lost on the fan who rushes to his seat to beat
the first pitch.*

                                        Thomas Boswell

Brian Doyle, Yankee Stadium, 1980

Three Cardinals, Shea Stadium, 1985

Marc Sullivan, Roger Clemens, and coach, Fenway Park, 1986

Singing the National Anthem, Tiger Stadium, 1986

Jim Rice, Fenway Park, 1986

Memorial Stadium, 1986

Anticipating cavalry, the organists assaults the score of the "Star Spangled Banner," which we attempt to sing because of the fierce joy that fills us and threatens to choke our throats unless we loosen a joyful noise. Then we chew the song's ending and lean forward to watch the young men assume the field in their vain uniforms, to hear "Play Ball," to allow the game's dance to receive our beings into its rhythms for two hours or three.

Donald Hall

Yankee Stadium, World Series, 1981

AFTERWORD

Baseball. It's only a game. But for many of us it is also a romance, one that often begins at an early age, and one that can last a lifetime. In these pages, Charles Kuralt recalls his introduction to baseball in the early 40's at Ponce de Leon Park in Atlanta. My first games were at Yankee Stadium in the early 60's. But our memories, it seems, are essentially the same. Perhaps surprisingly, the details of the games have mostly been forgotten, but the atmosphere, the moods and the rituals of baseball are remembered with great clarity.

Baseball's distinctive flavors, so rich in ambiance and tradition, in mannerism and affectation, engage our imagination and create the images and dreams of our childhoods. The game itself is so appealing, yet it is the culture of baseball that has enduring meaning in our lives.

This, I believe, is the magic of baseball, which lends itself to the printed word and has helped make baseball the writer's game. Yet, not often is baseball considered the photographer's game. Unlike other sports, where opposing players are constantly moving, blocking and colliding (making for dramatic action pictures), baseball's action is limited and sporadic. The players are spread out, and can rarely be photographed confronting each other in the same picture. Occasionally, there will be a great play at home, but chances are it won't happen when you're there.

But only baseball has the pre-game ritual. It is a time filled with the moods and romance of the sport. The players gracefully warm-up and take batting practice, reporters with cigars seek their daily quotes, some players joke and fool around while others sit alone in private moments of concentration. It is the time when player and fan meet.

For a photographer, the time before the game offers a chance to photograph baseball's world on an intimate scale. You can mingle around the batting cage, go in the dugouts and even — in certain situations — photograph in the clubhouse. All this provides an opportunity to photograph in a more personal style.

I visited baseball's world and photographed many times, but I tried not to become an insider; I tried to maintain a distance, to remain a fan and to experience the excitement. As a result, these pictures reflect my dreams of years ago.

Scott Mlyn

247